What people are saying about Behind Closed Doors.

Rothman and Derby bring a clarity and honesty to the craft of software-development management that I haven't felt since first reading Demarco and Lister's classic, *Peopleware*. Their story-based teaching style is engaging, and the tips contained provide a valuable reference for those who find themselves in the world of management.

► **Bil Kleb**
   Aerospace Engineering Manager, Washington, D.C.

I think you have a winner on your hands. I found the book extremely easy to read and understand, very relevant, and full of useful ideas and methods.

► **Andy Akins**
   Director of Development, TennesseeAnytime

After finishing each chapter, I felt like I could immediately apply the techniques in my daily work. After reading the entire book, I felt like everything came together and I could handle most day-to-day situations better.

► **Eric Roberts**
   Project Manager, Austin, Texas

How wonderful to have a window into the office of a great manager! Johanna Rothman and Esther Derby have created a fantastic resource for managers by not just decribing techniques, but by then showing them in action.

► **Elisabeth Hendrickson**
   Quality Tree Software, Inc.

Behind Closed Doors
Secrets of Great Management

Behind Closed Doors
Secrets of Great Management

Johanna Rothman

Esther Derby

The Pragmatic Bookshelf
Raleigh, North Carolina   Dallas, Texas

Pragmatic Bookshelf

ISBN 0-9766940-2-6

Printed on acid-free paper with 85% recycled, 30% post-consumer content.

First printing, September 2005

Version: 2005-8-23

For Edward Rothman, my first management mentor. And for Mark, Shaina, and Naomi, for continuing to teach me that management is a two-way street.

For my husband, Jeff Lee. Jeff, I appreciate you for your unstinting support. And for Jack (our dog) who reminds me to leave work at a reasonable hour.

Contents

List of Figures

List of Sidebars

Foreword

Through my first quarter century of working with technical managers, I developed a bad habit of assuming that all technical managers were bad managers. Rothman and Derby, in their short and wise book, *Behind Closed Doors: Secrets of Great Management*, show that I was wrong.

Most of these "bad managers" were not bad at all. They were simply ignorant of what it took to be a good manager—let alone a great manager.

And why were they ignorant? Because in the first twenty-five years of the software business, they had no great managers from whom to learn their trade. Like all pioneers, they were breaking unplowed ground, which is always a tough job.

A few of these first-generation managers grew into great managers, just around the time Rothman and Derby arrived in the business. Entering a generation later than I, they were able to observe and work with some of these great managers and thus form a more positive image of how a good, or great, manager would behave.

For the next generation, they have been passing this knowledge to hundreds of new managers—and now they are passing it on to you, their fortunate reader.

If you are starting your management career, you no longer have to figure it all out for yourself. Oh, there will still be plenty of figuring for you to do, but with Rothman and Derby's pages in your hand, you won't be starting from scratch.

Many years ago, when I first took a management job in IBM, I was given a secret little book that was given only to managers. I was clueless about what it took to be a good manager, so I devoured the book—only to be disappointed.

While that secret little book held some management wisdom, none of it pertained explicitly to technical managers, so it was only moderately useful to me. And some of it was just plain wrong for my kind of technical assignment.

All these years, I've been looking for something better to reveal the "secrets of great management" to the beginner (and more than a few old-timers). With *Behind Closed Doors*, my quest is over.

It was worth waiting for.

Jerry Weinberg
Computer Pioneer
August 2005

Preface

The first questions you might ask yourself when thumbing through a book on management are, "Who are these people? Are they for real? Or are they just a couple of consultants without a clue?"

We most definitely are for real. In fact, your authors have more than forty years' experience in management roles, across a wide variety of environments. We have managed or coached a variety of product development teams, functional teams, cross-functional teams, Agile teams, and operational teams. And over the years, we've noticed something important: most managers in technical organizations start the same way we did—as technical people.

Some people tell us that management doesn't matter—good technical people will produce results regardless of the quality of management. That has not been our experience. Poor managers create the illusion of productivity through busy-ness. Average managers finish work (but not always the right work). Great managers accomplish goals and develop people. As a result, we believe the quality of management makes a huge difference in bottom-line results and quality of work life.

Yet we've noticed that while there's lots of emphasis on technical training, there isn't much attention paid to training managers in technical organizations.

In a tiny minority of companies, newly minted managers receive management training and coaching to help them make a successful transition into a management role. More often, new managers receive a basic orientation and a high-level introduction on what to do—but don't receive much information on *how* to do it.

Sadly, many new managers receive no training at all—they are on their own to learn how to manage by observation, trial, and error. This method may save money in the training budget, but those savings are more than offset by lower productivity for the organization and personal stress for the manager and the group.

We believe that most new managers (and managers who have been in their positions for a while) want to do a good job but don't always know how to do a good job. Some of them have never seen good management—so how could they possibly be ready to be effective managers?

It doesn't have to be this way.

We decided to turn our experience and observations into a book to help managers see how to become great.

We've deliberately created a short timeline for this book. One of our reviewers asked, "Is this timeline science fiction?" It's not. A manager who knows how to apply a handful of management practices effectively can accomplish a great deal in a relatively short time. What we're showing in this book follows how we have organized our work as managers whether we were employees, contract managers, or management coaches: make contact with the people, learn what work people are doing, prioritize the work, and develop people through feedback and coaching.

If you don't know what people are doing, you can't organize the project portfolio. And if you can't organize the project portfolio, you can't know whether the work is being done well and on time, whether your group can take on more work, or whether you need more people. You just don't know. And that's just not acceptable for a manager.

We've written this book from the perspective of a talented mid-level manager, Sam. (Why show a bad example? We have enough of those!) We want to show you, our readers, how to coach people into performing management jobs, as well as show what a management job might look like. Some first-level managers may have more strategic work than Sam has; some mid-level managers may have less. Either way, every management role is unique, and the boundaries depend on the individual and the organization. But all managers have similar operational work; we want to show both first- and mid-level managers performing that work.

We've chosen to show a functional organization, one where each manager has responsibility for a layer of the product and where it's necessary to organize across groups to deliver product—a common structure for a development organization. You may work as part of a matrixed group of managers (where each function has a manager, and people from each function are assigned on a project basis). Or you may work in an organization that's using self-organizing teams and Agile methods. Every organization has its own spin on how to organize, but much of the management work remains the same.

If you're not sure of that, ask yourself who's responsible for the coaching and career development and for the feedback to the technical staff in your organization. And, ask yourself who monitors the development team *as a system*. The person who performs that work has a management role. We have a bias toward Agile project teams, because the team manages its own work—assigning responsibility for tasks, monitoring progress, solving problems—and frees the manager to work on removing obstacles that impede the team and solving broader problems. But we've seen many functional teams and matrixed teams be successful when they have effective managers. And we believe that the practices described and shown in this book can be adapted and applied to most situations.

You may notice one topic that often comes up in management books is missing in our book: leadership. To be honest, we don't buy the argument that leadership is different from management. We believe effective management and leadership are inextricable— and that great managers leave room for many people to exhibit leadership, rather than accreting leadership into one role. And on one level, leadership is a moot point: people who are not operationally savvy—who can't get things done—are neither managers nor leaders.

We thank our reviewers for their invaluable help: Andy Akins, Allan Baruz, David Bock, Paul Brown, Pascal Cauwenberghe, Dale Emery, Shae Erisson, Marc Evers, Elisabeth Hendrickson, Bil Kleb, Frederic Laurentine, Dwayne Phillips, Barb Purchia, Rob Purser, Eric Roberts, Bert Rodiers, Ellen Salisbury, Dave W. Smith, Mike Stok, Thomas Wagner, Jerry Weinberg, and Don Willerton. We'd especially like to thank our editor, Andy Hunt, for his help and support. Working with Andy and Dave at the Pragmatic Bookshelf has been a great experience. We couldn't have done it without you.

Johanna Rothman   *Esther Derby*
Arlington, MA   *Minneapolis, MN*

Introduction

Most of us have seen bad management at work, and you might learn what *not* to do by watching bad management. But to be a great manager, avoiding what not to do isn't good enough—great managers actively learn the craft of management.

It's worth learning how to be a great manager—both in human and in economic costs. The costs of bad management are enormous; we've been in numerous situations where we've seen the company fold because the managers couldn't manage their groups effectively.

Because managers amplify the work of others, the human costs of bad management can be even higher than the economic costs. We've seen people who were invaluable to the organization leave because they refused to work with poor managers—managers who depressed morale and productivity. We've talked to people who describe treatment that borders on abuse, meted out as "management."

Learning to be a great manager by yourself isn't easy—even if you carefully observe great managers. One of the reasons good management is so hard to learn is that much of management takes place behind closed doors. Generally speaking, you can observe only the public behaviors of managers and how your managers interact with you.

But managers interact with people of all personalities, skill levels, and motivations. And since those interactions often take place in private one-on-one meetings and in conference rooms where managers work together, the work is invisible to the rest of the world and to people aspiring to management.

We're going to open those doors and allow you to see great management in action.

Instead of preaching rules of management and innundating you with bullet points and checklists, we're going to open those closed doors and show you firsthand how a great manager handles the normal, day-to-day challenges and crises that arise. Our great manager is Sam.

As we begin our story, Sam Morgan has just taken the new position of Director of Development in a high-tech organization. Sam is in his midforties and has been managing groups of technical people for more than ten years. He's pretty sure everyone wants to do a good job, but it seems they don't always know what to do or how to do it. His job is to make sure everyone in his department—including the managers—knows what they need to do and that they have the right tools to do their jobs. Four managers report to Sam.

Ginger O'Brien is in her late twenties. This is her first management job, heading up the User Interface (UI) department. She is ambitious, excited about her work, and sure that there's one right way to do anything—even if she doesn't know that way yet.

Kevin McCloud manages the Middleware department. He's in his early thirties. He's tired. He slogs through the days, trying to keep up with all the work. He's sure if he just works hard enough, he'll succeed.

Jason Stone manages the Backend group but has extra responsibilities toward the Operations group. He has been managing people and projects for five years. He feels responsible for the Operations people, because they were part of his group until just a few months ago.

Finally, Patty Larsen manages the Database group. She's filling in as an acting manager as a favor to the previous director. She's in her midtwenties, and she's frustrated with being a manager. She wants to return to working as a technical lead.

We'll follow Sam over the course of his first weeks on the job. Watch as Sam works with his managers to create an effective and productive department, despite the usual array of difficulties.

What do you think Sam will do first?

Week One
Learning about the People and the Work

Some people think management is all about the people, and some people think management is all about the tasks. But great management is about leading and developing people and managing tasks.

If you want to lead people, you need to know them: their unique strengths, aspirations, and patterns of behavior. If you want to manage work, you need to see what people are doing and understand how it fits into the context of the group's mission.

You need to learn three things when you enter a new organization or job:

- Who the people are—their strengths and interests—and what they are working on

- The stated mission of the group and how the group provides value

- How your group fits into the larger organization

It would be great to learn this informations on your first day and in nice neat boxes. But it doesn't work that way; the information will emerge and coalesce as you uncover information and perform management work. Start with the people first in order to build trust and lay the foundation for a cohesive team. A good way to do this is to meet one-on-one with everyone who reports to you.

◇◇◇

Monday Morning

Ginger, the UI manager, arrived for her first one-on-one with Sam, breathless and three minutes late.

"Come on in and sit down, Ginger," Sam said.

"What's this meeting for? Our old manager never did this," Ginger said, as she flipped her red ponytail over her shoulder and plunked herself down in the chair. Crossing her arms, she leaned back.

"I like to meet with my direct reports every week."

"Oh. What do you want me to say?" Ginger asked.

"For this week, I'd like to get to know you better. Tell me a little about yourself." Sam opened his notebook and looked at Ginger, calm and alert.

Sam led the conversation to learn how Ginger worked and felt about her job. He used open-ended questions such as "How did you come to be in this job?" "What do you enjoy about your job?" and "What aspects are frustrating?" to tease out the information.

When Ginger declared she didn't have enough people to keep up with Marketing's "ever-changing demands," Sam decided to probe for more information.

"Tell me more about the ever-changing Marketing demands you mentioned. What's going on with that?"

As Sam asked more questions, he began to develop an understanding of how Ginger was working with the Marketing group—and how she wasn't.

When Sam felt he had heard enough to grasp the situation, he switched to a topic he always covered when he started with a new group.

"Are there any personnel or pay issues for you or anyone in your group?"

Ginger shrugged. "No, I'm happy, and as far as I know, my staff is happy too."

Sam and Ginger spent the rest of their half hour together talking about the projects Ginger's group was working on.

As he brought the meeting to a close, Sam asked, "Is there anything I missed?" Ginger shook her head. "Okay, how does this time work for you to set up a regular weekly one-on-one meeting?"

"You mean we're going to meet every week?"

"Yup. Every week," said Sam.

"Okay, this is as good as any day," Ginger acquiesced.

"Thanks for taking time to meet with me. If you think of anything else that I should know, or you have any question for me or about me, drop by."

By the end of the day, Sam had met with all four managers. He learned that Ginger, the UI manager, had hair that matched her name and her temperament. Kevin, the Middleware manager, was a nice fellow—very technical—but Sam wasn't sure how Kevin organized and prioritized the work for his group. Jason, the Backend manager, had his hands full with the Backend group supporting Operations as well as coaching his son's hockey team.

Patty, the Database manager, was hard to read. She'd answered questions but hadn't volunteered much.

Sam had seen a common theme emerge: everyone claimed he or she had too much to do and needed more staff.

Managing One Person at a Time

Properly done, one-on-ones build relationships. Managers who use one-on-one meetings consistently find them one of the most effective and productive uses of their management time.[1] One-on-ones provide a venue for coaching, feedback, career development, and status reporting.

One-on-one meetings will help your staff know what you expect of them and that you value them enough to spend time with them.

Establish a standard weekly time. Meet with each person on your staff at the same time every week. A standing meeting creates its own rhythm and helps both parties remember to be prepared.

Remember your manners. Don't take or make phone calls, return pages, or do other work during a one-on-one meeting. Allowing interruptions sends the message that your staff member isn't worth even a half hour of your uninterrupted time.

Hold one-on-ones faithfully. Canceling one-on-ones sends the message that you don't value your staff member,[6] and you will quickly lose touch with what's going on in the department. Persist with one-on-ones so you won't be surprised by late projects, unhappy employees, or festering problems.

Follow a consistent format for your one-on-ones. Consistency helps your staff know what to expect, how to prepare, and where to raise their issues.[3] This doesn't mean you have to use the same format for every person and stick to the format in the face of unusual events. But maintaining consistency across time allows people to see you as solid and reliable, not capricious. See *Making One-on-Ones Work* on page 150 for a suggested structure for productive one-on-ones.

Be adaptable. Meeting consistently is useless if you aren't also adaptable in how you interact and respond to people. Adapt your management style to the *individual* and be fair in how you handle *situations*.[2] Meet weekly with newer people or those who tend to veer off-track. Consider meeting every other week with people who plan their work, communicate proactively, and stay on-track.

That said, sometimes holding a weekly meeting sends the wrong message. If your group is responding to a crisis—one where the life of the organization is on the line—postpone one-on-ones for a short time. If crisis becomes a way of life, then return to regular one-on-ones. Regular one-on-ones help create a stable relationship between managers and team members, and help you learn about problems early. Learning about problems early leads to early solutions instead of crisis management.

Tuesday Morning

Sam started the day by making appointments to meet with his counterparts in other departments.

He called the Director of Marketing and left this message: "Sam Morgan here. I want to introduce myself. I started yesterday. I'm just learning the lay of the land. I'd like to set up a time to

You Can't Spend Too Much Time with People

After one of our management talks, a fellow approached us with a frown on his face. "You say I should meet with everyone weekly. Well, I have ten people on my staff, and if I met with every one of them every week, that would be five hours a week!" He was building up a head of steam. "That's almost a full day! If I spend all that time with people, I won't have time for my management work!"

Spending time with people *is* management work.

Budgets may count Full-Time Equivalents (FTEs), but great teams count on *people*. People are not fungible producers or FTEs. Great managers know this and learn about the people in their groups—their strengths, weaknesses, desires, and pressures.

We're not suggesting sitting in someone's office all day every day, watching over their shoulders. That's annoying micromanagement at best, productivity-reducing interference at worst. And we aren't suggesting prying into people's private lives and discussing their private decisions.

We are suggesting holding one-on-ones every week to learn about the people who report to you. Learn where they're successful. Learn what they don't want to do. Learn where their aspirations lie. Show an interest in who they are as people.

Establish office hours—a specific time each day (or a few days each week) set aside for drop-in visits.

Talk to people. Interact when there's no "reason" to interact. One manager we know noticed that team members started stopping by her office more often when she started keeping a stash of chocolate on her desk. Another manager set up a gumball machine outside his door (which is rarely closed).

Show an interest in the people who report to you as people. When we talk to people who say they have a great manager, one of the first statements we hear is, "She (or he) cares about me as a person."

meet with you in a week or so when I have more information about what's going on in this department." He also made an appointment with his boss, the VP of Product Development and the Director of Operations.

At 10:30 Tuesday morning, Sam had a half hour to walk around the department. He wanted to hear the tone of conversations and feel the mood and energy of the people. Even though Sam had a "getting to know you" pizza lunch scheduled for everyone in the department at the end of the week, he wanted to meet people before that.

As Sam wandered through the department, he stopped and chatted with the folks he'd met on the first day and introduced himself to those he hadn't met yet.

When Sam arrived at Jason's area, he heard yelling and went to investigate. Two developers faced off in front of a blank whiteboard.

"You erased my design! I have no idea what to do now!" a sandy-haired developer said, pointing his finger.

"What do you mean? You erased mine first!" the other shouted, tossing the eraser back in the tray.

Sam interrupted. "Hi, I'm Sam Morgan. I'm the new director. Something I can help with?"

"Give me my own whiteboard," the sandy-haired developer muttered, "so I don't have to share with other people," gesturing toward his teammate.

"Sounds like you guys are under the gun. What's up?"

The two developers explained that they were working on two high-priority fixes that affected the same module. Each person needed to see the other's design to ensure the designs didn't conflict. One had erased the other's design.

"Do you guys need more whiteboards?" Sam asked.

The developers looked at each other. "Maybe. Bigger whiteboards would work."

Sam jotted down a note to himself: Ask Jason about some new printing whiteboards—more whiteboards—bigger whiteboards?

Don't Offer Help If You Can't Deliver

We recently heard a story about a manager who wanted to help his staff. "You're doing work critical to the company's success. Can I help you in any way?"

One of the developers said, "Sure. How about three more people so we can finish this faster?" The manager frowned and said, "Sorry, can't do that."

Another developer said, "Hey, we're stuck working on these old machines no one else wanted. It would be great if you could replace these machines with the newest model? The new machines would be about twenty times faster."

The manager frowned again, and said, "Sorry, no budget."

Another developer asked for focused time for assistance from the architect. "Sorry, can't do that either. His new project is critical, too."

The developers stopped asking for help. The moral of this story is: Don't offer help if you can't deliver it.

"I'll let you guys get back to work," Sam said, and continued on his rounds. Sam wandered through the department, stopping to chat here and there, asking questions, and jotting notes in his notebook.

When Sam returned to his office, he flipped through his notes.

Everyone is working way too hard and too long.
Empty pizza boxes and take-out boxes from
last night's dinner.
People seem to be reacting strongly to small events,
like erasing a diagram on a whiteboard.
On the other hand, the people respect each other,
and morale seems good.

◇◇◇

Keep a Finger on the Pulse

There's an exception to management behind closed doors. Management by Walking Around and Listening (MBWAL) is an informal technique that helps managers use their five senses to gauge the mood and energy of the group.[5] Along with one-on-ones, MBWAL is part of your early warning system to detect when people are over-stressed or morale is slipping so you are not blindsided. MBWAL allows managers to observe the clues about how work really happens and how the culture is evolving.

Part of being good at MBWAL is cultivating a curious mind, always observing, and questioning the meaning of what you see.

Respect people's space and time. Be careful not to interrupt people. When a person is on the phone or concentrating on work, scram. If the person is free, pause and chat for a minute or two. Ask carefully. Some questions are can be open to misinterpretation: "What are you doing?" or even "How's it going?" can give the impression of micromanagement, especially if people are working under deadlines. Try a neutral question such as: "What's up?"

Even better than a neutral question is a helping question: "Do you need anything?" or "Any obstacles you need me to remove?" The context and culture in your organization and your relationships will drive how people interpret your questions. If you feel the need to spend more than a few minutes with any one person, make an appointment to follow up.

And it goes without saying, but if you offer help, you need to follow through and provide the help requested, or people will be disinclined to ask again.

Take notes. If someone has a specific request, write it down immediately. Record other observations back in your office—people may become suspicious of you if you wander around taking notes without talking. Use a notebook to record observations. Over time, your notes will help you see patterns, both in your organization and in the way you manage.

Be careful about demos. Sometimes, people will be so excited about what they are working on they'll want to show you. This is great! But asking for an impromptu demonstration of the product shows disrespect for the other person's time.

◇◇◇

Wednesday Afternoon

On Wednesday afternoon, Sam sent this email to the management team:

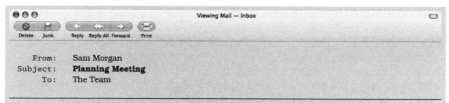

From: Sam Morgan
Subject: **Planning Meeting**
To: The Team

It was great to meet you earlier this week and learn about the work you're doing.

One of the themes I heard is that we're understaffed, and we need more people to meet the release date. This is an issue that we need to work on together as a management team.

I'm concerned this is going to sound like I'm piling more work on you when you already have a ton of work. And if we don't plan as a department, we won't know where to add people and we won't escape this crunch.

I'm scheduling a two-hour meeting for Friday afternoon so we can see the big picture of all the work.

To prepare for the meeting, please create a list for your group of all the work currently underway or planned for the next 3-4 weeks. Include the following:

- A list of everyone in your group and what they are working on. Name specific projects where you can.

- Any promised deliverables to other groups that are due in the next 3-4 weeks.

- A list of periodic work (e.g., reports, maintenance, upgrades)

- A list of ongoing work (e.g., support, database tuning)

I'd like to see as complete a list as possible of all the work going on in our department. Until we–as a management team–see all the work everyone in the department is doing, we can't make good decisions about where and when we need more people. We'll use this information to create a matrix so we can see who's doing what for the next month. If you have questions about what I'm asking for, send me a note or stop in before the meeting.

The meeting will be in Conference Room A at 3 PM on Friday.

Sam

Friday Afternoon

Sam arrived at Conference Room A at 2:55. When he entered the room, Patty was already there, with her head in a book.

Patty looked up. "Oh, hi. I was taking advantage of a few quiet minutes to review my problem set for tomorrow's class."

"Oh, your class for your degree?" Sam asked, as he started covering the wall with flip-chart paper.

"Yep, it's a challenge to do all my class work and my work work," Patty sighed, as she closed her book and gathered up her notes.

Jason strolled in, folders in hand. "I'm ready for this. I've got the lists of everything that's going on in my group."

Kevin shuffled in after Jason. He griped, "My group is overloaded. I've been helping out, but there's still too much to do." He plunked himself down at the conference table. "But don't worry, we will do what we need to do."

At 3:05 PM, Ginger arrived in a flurry. "Sorry I'm late," she called. "Meetings!"

"Yep, we all love meetings. Let's get started on this one. We're here to figure out all the work we as a group have to do and what we can't do right now," Sam said. "I've drawn a matrix up here on the wall."

"I know I need more people!" Ginger blurted out.

Sam nodded to Ginger. "We're going to look at all our work and determine how to proceed as a team," Sam responded.

"I'd like each of you to fill in this matrix with the work your teams are doing. I've listed the names of everyone in the area, grouped by functional area. Let's start by listing each person's tasks for the next three weeks. Who wants to go first?"

"I'll go," said Ginger. Ginger strode to the wall, list in hand. She filled in 'GUI Coding' across all four weeks for six of her people. For the other two, she listed 'Focus Groups' for Week 1 and 2 and 'GUI Coding' for Week 3 and 4.

"Can you be more specific than 'GUI coding'?" asked Sam. Ginger looked surprised. "More specific? But 'GUI coding' *is* what they're

Week1
(this week)   Week2   Week3   Week4

UI
Judy
Roger
Henny
Middleware
Eli
Adam
Hannah
Backend

Database

Figure 1.1: START OF A PORTFOLIO

---

doing. My team is hard at work writing GUI code based on the marketing requests. I trust that they're doing the right thing."

"I didn't mean to imply you don't trust your people. We need the detail so we can understand what everyone is doing and what the priorities are. Is any of this work for previous releases or future releases?"

"I'll have to get back to you on that," Ginger said.

Kevin volunteered to go next. "We're always crunched in Middleware," he said. Kevin started listing the work for his group. "There are four major projects in my group. I assign everyone 25% to each project." Kevin wrote small to fit the four project titles into each box. Sam said, "How do people know what to work on first when they're working on four projects at the same time?"

"They juggle," Kevin frowned, puzzled by Sam's question.

"How about you, Jason?" Sam asked.

Multitasking: Wasting Mental Cycles

Working on two tasks (not projects or teams) can improve productivity because when a person is stuck on one task, they can switch to the other. While they're working on the second task, their unconscious mind is still processing the first and may come up with a bright idea. People working on two tasks at a similar level of detail can be more productive because they aren't sitting idle and the similar tasks may be synergistic.

Productivity may increase when a person has two related tasks, but it plummets as the number of *projects* increases.

Each task switch takes time—time to mentally put things away and tie up loose ends, time to re-create a train of though, reorganize and reset. Add enough tasks, and pretty soon most of the time goes to switching, not doing productive work.

And time is the one asset you can never reclaim.

Jason stood up and started filling in the work for his group. "I'm going to have to double-check this. My list is based on last month's status report."

Jason broke down the work as 50% support and 50% development and wrote notes for each one. "I've got two people working on development, and the other seven are working on reports when they aren't on support issues."

"We can work with what you have now, but for the next round we'll need an up-to-date task list. What's driving the support?" Sam asked.

Jason grimaced. "A lot of it's leftover from the last release. We're helping the Operations people through some manual workarounds and finishing a couple of features that we implemented halfway in the last release."

Patty was the last to approach the wall. "I only have one week of work to post. I have four people who are reliable and can do what they take on. But the other three—I just can't tell with them. So, I evaluate the work every week to see whether I need to reassign it.

"That's a tough nut to crack. Let's talk about that in our one-on-one this week." Sam stood and turned to the board.

"We've made great progress today, and we need more details. I'm going to schedule another meeting to continue this work. Let me review our actions from this meeting. These are the items we need to have completed before the next meeting.

"Ginger, you're going develop more specific descriptions of your group's work, yes?" Ginger nodded.

"Kevin, you're going to find out how people determine what to work on first." Kevin dipped his head.

"Jason, you're going to break down the support and development into more specific tasks, right?

"Patty, you define all the work your group can complete in the next three weeks, and we'll deal with the work assignment later.

"We have our one-on-ones scheduled for Monday, so we can talk more about your specific situations in those meetings. I'll schedule the follow-up meeting to continue this work on Tuesday. I'll take the flip charts back to my office with me, and we can continue working with our matrix when we reconvene."

As Sam met with each of his managers on Monday, he coached them on how to develop a more detailed picture of the work in their groups. Patty and Ginger decided to talk to everyone individually because people in their groups worked on small, independent projects. Kevin decided to gather the data in a group meeting—his team's work was interdependent. Jason chose to meet separately with his two groups because their work was different in nature: one group worked on development, and the other supported deployed products.

When Sam met with Patty, he discovered another problem. Patty didn't want to be a manager. She explained that she'd agreed to move into the management role temporarily, and wanted to return to technical work. Sam and Patty scheduled a meeting to discuss the move. Until she transitioned, Sam knew he'd need to coach Patty to perform the management work in her group.

◇◇◇

Gather Data about Current Work

It's common for unsanctioned, unfunded, and unneeded work to slip into what your group is doing. Until you know all the work your group is doing and how your group adds value to the organization, you can't make good decisions about priority, what work to do, and what work not to do.[4]

Understand what people are actually doing. Gather information from each person in your group. Understand all the work that they do: project work, ad hoc work, periodic work, ongoing work, and management work.

- Project work has a start and an end and meets specific organizational goals.

- Ad hoc work is work that appears to come from nowhere— a crisis, an unanticipated request, or other work that wasn't planned.

- Ongoing work keeps the business and the operation running.

- Periodic work happens at predictable intervals.

- Management encompasses the planning and organization of the rest of the work.

Management work also includes hiring, developing, and retaining people; budgeting; reporting; influencing; and creating value through the work of the group.

This constitutes the "universe of work" for your group.

Create a big visible chart of the work. Use a whiteboard or wall to lay out all the work in a matrix. Having all the work visible and in front of people helps them see the big picture and patterns.

Iterate. The first time you do this, you won't have all the information you need. Keep digging. Generic tasks such as "coding" or "testing" provide insufficient information. Focus on the results of an activity and how those results provide value to the business. Questions such as "Who will use this?" "When do they need it?" and "What's the result if you don't provide it?" help people articulate the level of detail needed to prioritize the work.

Understand resistance. Sometimes people are reluctant to tell you what they are actually working on. They may feel you are micromanaging them or don't trust them. They may fear that they'll have to give up work that's valuable to them but not the organization. (You will.) Keep plugging. Help people understand the big picture— why certain work is important and how it fits into the organization's goals. Be willing to listen: your staff may know something you don't know.

Now Try This

- Initiate weekly one-on-ones with each person in your group. Use the guidelines shown in *Making One-on-Ones Work* on page 150.

- Notice someone doing something well, and comment on it.

- Leave your office! The key to MBWAL is to notice changes. Become familiar with the normal noise level, décor, and mood. Don't limit yourself to the office area. Stop for coffee in the kitchen area. Eat lunch with in the lunchroom. Take a look at *Manage by Walking Around & Listening* on page 142 for more ideas.

- Make a list of all the work your group performs, including your own. Use the list to start a project portfolio for the group.

Bibliography for Chapter

[1] Kenneth Blanchard and Spencer Johnson. *The One Minute Manager*. Berkeley Publishing Group, New York, 1982.

[2] W. Steven Brown. *Thirteen Fatal Errors Managers Make and How You Can Avoid Them*. Berkley Books, New York, 1985.

[3] Esther Derby. "What Your Weekly Meetings Aren't Telling You." *Better Software*, volume 3(6):pages 40–41, March 2004.

[4] Peter Drucker. *Managing for Results*. Pan Books, London, 1964.

[5] Thomas J. Peters and Robert H. Jr. Waterman. *In Search of Excellence: Lessons from America's Best-Run Companies*. Warner Books, New York, 1982.

[6] Johanna Rothman. "No More Meeting Mutinies." *Software Development*, March 2002.

Week Two
Bringing Order to the Chaos

There's almost always more work than people to do it. It's impossible to do everything. Set clear priorities, and choose to do the work that is most important.

The principles are the same for product companies and IT organizations: understand what everyone is working on, articulate priorities, and choose only the work that supports the goals of the group and the organization.

Chaos hides problems—both with people and projects. When chaos recedes, problems emerge. As a manager, you can choose how to resolve them, and resolve them you must.

◇◇◇

Tuesday Afternoon

On Tuesday afternoon, the management team reconvened. "Where do I put the projects I can't cover?" Ginger asked.

"Let's make a flip chart for unstaffed work," Sam replied. "We'll write the work down the side and the weeks across. write the number of people you think you need each week for that work, and we'll see where and when we're short-staffed."

Each manager went to the board in turn and filled in the details for the current work and plans for the next three weeks. Each added to the list of unstaffed work.

UNSTAFFED WORK

Project/task	Week 1	Week 2	Week 3
Order vantry (O.E.) changes—UI	2	2	
O.E. changes middleware	1	1	2
O.E. backend		1	1

Figure 2.1: SHOWING UNSTAFFED WORK IN A PROJECT PORTFOLIO.

"Now that we've got the full list, let's look at how all the work maps to our department goals. When I took this job, Marty, my boss, told me to reduce our operations costs and improve revenue.

"Before you start thinking 'layoff,' let me reassure you that no one has mentioned staff reduction to me." Sam could see the relief on people's faces. Sam wrote "reduce operations cost and improve revenue" on a flip chart and posted it where everyone could see it. "How does that match with the goals you've been working toward?"

Ginger exclaimed, "I'm just trying to keep Marketing off my back."

"I'm trying to keep Operations up and running so our customers are happy," Jason said.

Kevin said, "Every time Marketing wants an interface to some new database, we supply that."

Patty said, "We react to all the database changes."

Sam thought, *Here's another piece of the problem. Everyone has different goals, and individually those goals don't support reducing cost and improving revenue.*

"It sounds as if each of you is working toward a different goal," Sam said.

"Well, we all want to get the product out the door," Jason said. "And keep it out."

"Yes, you're right. It's partly about releasing product and keeping it out so the operations costs are lower. It's also about putting predictability into our release schedules so we can plan on revenue. Let's look at the work in the light of this mission. What work will help us achieve that goal?" asked Sam.

Jason started the conversation. "If our goal is to reduce operations costs, then the most important thing for my group is to fix the workarounds from the last release." Jason turned to Sam, "What if I stopped all development and assigned everyone to fixing the workarounds for the next three weeks? We could actually finish the workarounds from the last release in three weeks and free half my group to work on development for the next release."

"Let's make avoiding half-baked features a topic in our next management meeting," Sam agreed, and turned to Ginger. "Ginger, what about those focus groups? Are they supporting our departmental goal?" Sam asked.

"Well, we're using them for usability studies," Ginger said. "But I guess we could drop that for now."

"If you don't do the focus groups, does that change anything?" Sam asked.

"Sure does," agreed Ginger. "I can cover some of the unstaffed projects. Maybe all of them."

The group continued working through the list of work, creating a list of projects that didn't support the goal of improving revenue by reducing support costs. By the end of the meeting, they had a list of eight questionable projects.

"Okay, we've identified five projects we know we don't need to do and three that we may transition or cancel," Sam said. "Continue those three until I receive a definite answer from my boss. Redirect people to more important work for the five projects we know we're canning. Be sure to explain the reasoning. Otherwise, it will be hard for people to transition. We'll meet again Friday afternoon to hammer out the staffing."

The Fable of the Rising Young Manager

Once upon a time, there was a Rising Young Manager. He knew he was rising because he had twenty people in his group, including three technical leads who focused on accomplishing the day-to-day work of his group at his very capable direction.

But in spite of the three technical leads (and seventeen other people), there was never an end to all the work, and some Important Things did not get done at all. The three technical leads (and seventeen other people) commenced to grumble, and the Rising Young Manager felt rather peckish, too.

"With twenty people you should be able to accomplish all your high-priority work and then some," the Rising Young Manager's boss declared. "What you need is a consultant to help you whip those three technical leads (and seventeen other people) into Shape." And so a consultant was hired and arrived to help the Rising Young Manager whip the three technical leads (and seventeen other people) into shape.

When the consultant arrived, she asked the Rising Young Manager to explain all the work that the three technical leads (and seventeen other people) were doing.

"I have it all here, in a spreadsheet, along with assignments, start dates, and end dates for each project," the Rising Young Manager said, feeling some pride at the advanced state of his organizational system.

"I see you are working on thirty-five projects," the Consultant said. "That's a lot of work."

The Rising Young Manger beamed. "Indeed. You see, recently the company retired three of our fine products. We've been working with the people who use these fine products for years, and we won't leave them in the lurch."

The consultant rubbed her chin. "Your customer service ethic is admirable," she said. "And I suppose the personalized support you are providing—it's free of charge?"

(continued...)

She raised an eyebrow. The Rising Young Manager nodded. "Yes, I thought so," the Consultant continued, and made a note. "And they can comfortably continue with this retired product indefinitely?"

The Rising Young Manger nodded and looked pleased at the consultant's quick grasp of the situation.

"So the customers will be happy, but will they ever buy the new product that your company is desirous of selling now and thus bring revenue into your company?"

The Rising Young Manager thought for a moment, and his face fell. "I see you do not really understand customer service," he said. "I dismiss you."

After the consultant left, the Rising Young Manager crept to his office, closed his door, and carefully reviewed his spreadsheet. His face began to glow red. *"I have made an error,"* he thought to himself.

The very next day, the Rising Young Manager stopped all personalized support projects and some other pet projects, too. He reassigned two of the technical leads and several of the other seventeen people.

Suddenly, Important Things were getting done again, and the three technical leads and (seventeen other people) cheered up as they once again left work at a reasonable hour.

"That consultant really whipped things into shape" the Rising Young Manager's boss commented some time later.

"Well, I did most of it myself," the Rising Young Manager said modestly. "I don't allow distractions like unfunded projects and always focus on the overall company goals. I find that proper focus enables us to get done what needs doing."

"Ah, you are a young man who is sure to continue to rise," said the boss, as he smiled benevolently.

The moral of this fable is: Focus on the funded work.

(Like many fables, this is a true story.)

Create the Project Portfolio: Match the Work to the Goals

Every group or department has a mission—it's their reason for being and describes how they provide value to the organization. As organizations evolve, people take on work that makes sense at the time. As goals and priorities change, the work should change, too. As you start gathering information for your project portfolio, you'll see some work that no longer serves the department's goals.

Every organization we've ever been in has at least one report— usually one that eats scads of person hours—that ends up recycled because the mailstop no longer exists. The person who originally requested the report has moved (on, up, or out), and no one needs the report anymore. And this is just one obvious example. We're good at identifying the need for ongoing work, but often don't recognize when that need no longer exists.

Update your big visible chart. As you learn more about what's happening, update your big visible chart. Using a big visible chart for planning is useful. It helps everyone see the same picture at the same time. Keeping it up-to-date creates shared ownership and lets people see patterns and problems—and sometimes solutions. We often see people clustered around big visible charts talking about how the work fits together.

Clarify and communicate department goals. You can't make decisions about priority without understanding your department goals. Write your department goals on one page and post them prominently. Goals belong not just in management offices but also in the public spaces of your groups' work areas. Visible reminders keep people on-track, help people make good decisions, and make it everyone's job to challenge work (especially ad hoc work) that doesn't fit the department goals.

Don't fall into the trap of waiting for your manager to define department goals for you. Formulate goals that fit your understanding, and give them to your manager for feedback. You need to have some working set of goals to prioritize work and do your job effectively.[7]

Product or Force Behind the Product?

Working in a company that makes money from selling a software product is different from working in an IT group that supports a company that makes money from selling some other product or service. But not that different.

In a company that generates revenue by selling the software product your group participates in building, the connection between your work and the bottom line is clear. When you work in an IT group, the tie between your group and the bottom line may be less direct but it's still important.

The questions you ask to help define the mission of your group—and the strategically important work—have a different focus.

In a product company, ask these questions:

- How does the work of this group contribute to generating revenue?
- How does the work of this group attract new customers and keep existing customers?

In an IT group, ask these questions:

- How does the work of this group enable the company to do business (or to do more business more efficiently or effectively)?
- How does the work of this group affect the company's bottom line?
- How does the work of this group support the business unit's ability to generate revenue and continue business operations?

For both companies that sell software and companies that sell some other product or service, the focus is on generating revenue and attracting and retaining customers. A product group's mission will look different from an IT group's mission. Once you've defined the mission of your group, managing the work is actually quite similar.

Categorize all the projects. Once you have a complete list, review each project against your department's goals. Create four lists:

- Projects and work you know you will continue.

- Projects and work you know you need to stop—the "not-to-do" list. This is work that provides no value to anyone in the organization. Stop it now.

- Projects and work that may be important but may not fit in your group. This is work you can't just drop; transition it to a more appropriate group.

- Projects and work that you don't know where they fit. This is work that you aren't sure whether it's in the second or third category. Investigate before canceling or transitioning projects.

Discuss the last two lists with your manager to determine what to do. Work with your boss to reassign work that's not strategically important—work you shouldn't do.[9] Decide whether you need to continue performing that work until someone else takes it or whether you can just drop it. Make a conscious decision, and communicate it to your boss and other people who need to know.

Thursday

It had been three days since Sam learned Patty no longer wanted to manage—she wanted to be a database architect. He hadn't planned to replace a key member of his management team in the first month. But that's what he had to do.

Sam took a few minutes to gather his thoughts before his meeting with Patty. *This could go three different ways: Patty could want to stay in the group, find another job within the company, or leave the company altogether. I want her to stay, at least in the company. I want to make sure I cover these three topics in our meeting:*

- *Verify that she wants to leave management.*

- *Enlist her help in analyzing the manager's job.*

- *Determine what to do for the people who aren't delivering—I'm not sure they're lost causes.*

Stepping Back from Management

Management isn't for everyone. If you find it's not for you, or it's not for you *yet*, it's okay to step back into a technical role. Some people attach a stigma to "moving backward," but we've never seen anyone do long-term damage to their career. And, we've seen the stress level plummet both for the person who re-chose a technical role and the group they were managing.

If you're not convinced, ask successful technical managers in your organization about their career paths. If you probe, most managers will tell you they veered between technical leadership roles and technical management roles, not following a linear career progression.

In our work with managers, we have found that the best managers practice management and practice technical leadership, moving between both types of jobs before they decide to focus on one or the other.

Remember, technical management is about working with people, not technology. Sure, a component of the role is focused on technological decisions, but if you don't want to work with people in this organization or in this role, step back from management. Ask yourself these questions:

- Do I want to control more of the technical decisions?
- Am I more interested in fixing technical problems than people problems?

If you answered "yes" to both questions, you may be more comfortable in a technical leadership role than a people leadership role. You can always practice people skills in a technical role. This will give you information to see whether a people-oriented management role may fit in the future. If you think management might be for you, ask yourself:

- Do I like working with people?
- Do I like coaching and mentoring people?
- Am I willing to learn how to provide feedback and have difficult conversations with people when I need to?

If you answered "yes" to these questions, management may be a good fit for you, now or in the future. No one is born a great manager; it takes practice.

Sam looked up and saw Patty standing in his doorway. "Come on in, Patty."

Patty sat down and opened her notebook.

"I want to ask you again, now that you've had time to think about it: are you sure you want to move to an technical contributor role?" asked Sam.

Patty stared into space and then turned to him. "I never wanted to be a manager. I was supposed to be the interim manager while the old manager looked for a replacement. I love doing database architecture work, and I can't do that and be a manager, too."

"Let's talk for a few minutes about your career goals," Sam suggested.

Patty looked straight at Sam. "I want to do technical work. That's why I'm in school working on a master's. Management is not part of what I want to do right now."

"We'll need to prepare the group for the change," Sam said. "Even though you'll be in the same group, you'll be in a different role. That means the team will be reforming. And it may take some time for the team to see you as 'one of the guys' again."

"We need to hire a new manager." Sam said. "I'd like you to help me with that, and then we need to figure out how to help your current group to deliver more reliably."

Patty furrowed her brows.

"I'd hate to hire a new manager and put him or her in the situation of having to manage poor performance. Have you given feedback?"

Patty paused. "Well, sort of. That's the problem. I hate telling other people they aren't doing their job. I kind of told them. I mean, I hinted, but they didn't understand." She shook her head.

Sam thought, *I need to work with Patty on feedback. That's a separate conversation.*

"Would you like me to help you with this? It's important to let people know when their work isn't acceptable. I'd like you to give the actual feedback, but I'll coach you on what to say." Sam offered.

Patty looked relieved. "That would be great. Part of why it's hard to give feedback is I just don't know the words to say."

Sam

> Day-to-day management of Database group
> Project scheduling for the work
> Hiring, retention, firing
> Budget---capital and operations budgets
> Status reporting
> Project portfolio management
> Performance evaluations
> Results of one-on-one meeting issues with the Database staff

Ginger, Kevin, Roger

> Organizing the work of the group to deliver:
> Database architecture to support changes in the product
> Database generation to support new development and testing
> Database tuning
> Bug fixing

Test and support groups

> Organizing the work of the group to deliver:
> Cloning and creating databases for problem re-creation and testing

Database staff

> Hold one-on-one meetings
> Provide group goals
> Help individuals develop their goals
> Provide feedback
> Negotiate professional development plans

IT infrastructure

> Keep database servers up

Figure 2.2: PATTY'S LIST OF MANAGEMENT DELIVERABLES

"Let do that in your next scheduled one-on-one. Let's use the rest of our time to analyze your job. Let's start with you and make a list: who do you work with now, and what are your deliverables to them?"

Sam and Patty discussed her role and came up with the list in Figure 2.2.

Sam and Patty used the interactions and deliverables list to identify qualities, preferences, and non-technical skills necessary to succeed in the role. Then they discussed how technical the new manager needed to be. First they addressed the database technical skills and discussed how quickly the manager needed to be able to look inside the product and understand it. "This is very helpful. I can use this analysis to write a job description," said Sam. "Thank you," he said, smiling.

"Let's run this by the rest of the management team to see whether we missed anything. I'll take care of the paperwork with HR for your role change and for hiring a new manager," said Sam. "Then we'll start creating an interviewing team and looking for candidates."

Fast-Forward

With the help of the interviewing team, Sam evaluated candidates. At the end of three weeks, the best fit was clear. Sam made an offer to the top candidate, Brian. Sam and Patty continued to work on resolving the issues with the Database group so the new manager didn't walk into a mess.

Two weeks after receiving the offer, Brian started.

Patty walked to her car at the end of Brian's first day. She was exhausted, relieved, and just a little sad. *I didn't expect Brian's first day to be so hard on me. I'm happy I'm back to being a database architect, but it was starting to be fun working with Ginger, Kevin, and Jason as part of the management team. I'm going to miss that. Saying goodbye to that management team was hard.*

Matching the Roles with the People

Match strengths and talents with roles. No one can be successful when their skills and interests don't match their role. Many fine people look like "poor performers" because they are in the wrong role. Rather than force people to persevere in a role that doesn't fit, find a role that does fit.[3]

Provide feedback. Sometimes people aren't doing a good job, but no one has told them. Without that information, they not only don't know what to change, they don't know they need to change. Before you decide someone is a poor performer, examine how well

Skills are Only Part of the Equation

Most managers strive to hire capable people with the qualities, skills, and abilities to succeed. But people who seem like a good fit aren't always successful. And sometimes managers inherit staff who may not be the best fit for the jobs. Poor performance *might* be the result of insufficient skills. But it might be something else.

Performance also depends on the environment and the quality of management. Before you decide someone is a "poor performer," check that you're providing an environment in which this person can succeed. Ask yourself these questions:

- Have I communicated my priorities so that this person can make good decisions about what to do when?

- Have I checked to make sure he or she understands my expectations by asking the person to rephrase them in his or her own words?

- Have I been clear in making assignments—stating constraints and specific boundaries about the work?

- Have I provided feedback that was clear and specific so that this person could change to meet my expectations?

- Have I discussed options for gaining any necessary skills?

Suppose you've done all this, and the person still isn't providing the results you want. Look for factors in the environment—procedures, measures, and rewards—and system problems.

(continued...)

One company we know established a target metric for the length of support calls handled by help-desk staff. That worked for simple problems, but when a more complex call came in—one that took more time to resolve than the call limit—the help-desk staff members were penalized when they stayed on the phone long enough to solve a problem.

Another company had the habit of releasing software on tight deadlines. The tighter the deadline, the less time developers and testers had to prevent, detect, and fix problems, increasing technical debt. Each time, the manager intended to return to fix the technical debt. With every new release, there wasn't quite enough time. With each release, the code grew more brittle—and brittle code takes longer to modify. So, with each release, it was more difficult to make the deadline, and the technical debt increased. Making changes to the code grew more difficult and more error prone. Anyone working in that part of the code looked bad, because his or her code was prone to break.

One of the mistakes managers make is labeling environmental and system problems as individual problems—and then firing the poor performer. But if the problem is an environment problem or system problem, the problem doesn't disappear when the "poor performer" does.

you've done at set clear expectations, set reasonable interim deliverables, and communicated your satisfaction (or dissatisfaction) with the quality of results. See *Guide to Giving Effective Feedback* on page 134 for more details.

Hire the best. Ideally, you start with a good fit by hiring the right person for the job. Hiring is the most important decision a manager can make.[10] When hiring, the greater the span of influence for the position, the more critical the decision. We think hiring is so important that even though we told the story of hiring Patty's replacement in a few paragraphs, we're going to present the steps for you here. For an in-depth treatment, see Johanna's book.[10]

Analyze the job. Before you start advertising for any candidates, understand exactly what it is you want them to do. "Management" is not an adequate job description. Prepare for hiring by analyzing the job and writing a job description. Make the description as specific as you can[1] but not so constrained that HR filters out good candidates.

Here's an example of an overconstrained job description: "Expertise in multi-threaded applications, real-time embedded systems, transaction processing systems, managing twelve-to-fifteen person development teams, leaps tall buildings in a single bound." You are not likely to find someone (anyone!) who can do all of these tasks well.

Source candidates. Use a variety of sources to find qualified candidates. Your company's website, other job boards, personal networking, advertising, and job fairs are great places to find candidates. If you are having trouble finding candidates, use an external recruiter—people who know how to look for the sort of candidate you seek.

Winnow the candidates. As résumés arrive, read and screen for the people who are the mostly likely fit. We sort résumés into three piles: Yes, No, and Maybe. Phone screen the people in the Yes pile right away. If you don't have enough candidates after the phone screen, move to the Maybes. Let people in the No pile know you aren't interested.

Develop behavior description questions. Behavior description questions such as "Tell me about a time when..." help candidates explain how they've worked in the past rather than how they *wish* they work.[8] Hypothetical questions such as "What would you do if..." don't uncover how people really act.

Phone screen before in-person interviewing. Especially for management candidates, consider the *dirtbag* phone screen:[6] have an administrator or other nonmanagement person call to confirm basic data such as employment dates and availability for a more in-depth phone screen. Good management candidates will be pleasant to everyone they speak with in the interview process, not just the hiring manager.

Develop an audition. An audition gives you a chance to see a candidate in action, performing a small piece of the job.[5] Management auditions might include negotiating for resources, changing a schedule, hiring, facilitating a meeting, providing feedback, delivering unwelcome news, or some other aspect of management.[10] Auditions are particularly useful to see skills in action.

If the position has substantial technical content, a "vague design question" is a useful technique. Listen for the candidate to ask clarifying questions. Watch for the candidate to defend a poor design in the face of feedback or new information. Probe for the candidate to understand and acknowledge trade-offs.

Interview candidates with an interview team. Set up one-on-one interviews between the candidate and each member of the interview team. Avoid having the candidate answer the same question several times, unless you are looking for consistency in the answers.

Panel interviews seem like they will save time, but they require substantial coordination and practice to be effective. Further, panel interviews feel like the Inquisition to the candidate.

Involve as many people as possible when selecting new team members and team leaders. The more people who interview the candidate, the less likely you and your group are to make a mistake in hiring. The fewer people involved, the more likely you are to miss aspects of a candidate.

Listen to the interview team's assessment. Once the interviews are complete, gather the interview team for an evaluation meeting,[6] where each can share his or her impressions of each candidate. As a manager, you have final say on who is hired. Listen to the opinion of the group. Override their opinion at your peril.[10]

Check references. Once you've identified the candidate you want for the job, check references. Take the reference opportunity to confirm the wonderful information you've heard from the candidate (and to discuss possible red flags).[10]

Extend an offer. Work with HR to develop an appropriate offer, including salary, benefits, bonus, vacation, and other particulars as defined by your company. Make your offer with an expiration date so you aren't left hanging as the candidate mulls over his options for weeks.

Plan to Integrate New Team Members

You can speed up the integration of new people—or the same people in new roles—by planning for the transition. Start with the basics: without a place to sit, a phone, and access to email, a new hire is invisible to the organization.

Create and use a checklist for new hires. Use the checklist on page 136 to verify you've addressed the logistics. Have the new hire's office ready on the first day.

Spend time setting the context on the first day. Discuss your specific context with the person in transition: the product, the departmental goals and especially how that person's work fits into those goals.[2]

Assign a buddy. Especially with a new hire, assign someone who can show the person where the cafeteria, coffee, supplies, and restrooms are.[10] Have the buddy walk the person through the technical pieces of the job, too.

Expect to re-form teams. Anytime team membership changes, you have a new team. You may need to revisit some earlier stages of team formation—albeit briefly. Give the team time and support to become productive again.

Friday Morning, Sam's Second Week on the Job

On Friday morning, the group reconvened in Conference Room A. Sam posted the flip chart from the previous week on the wall.

"I'm glad we did this with stickies," enthused Jason. "We've got a lot of changes to make."

"Before we start, let's make sure we agree on our most important projects," Sam said.

Sam led the discussion to establish priority for features and fixes. For each feature and current high-priority fixes, they discussed the business value and business impact, the risk, and the costs to implement. "That's good enough for now. Next time we'll include Marketing. And, we'll review the lower-priority fixes then. I'm meet-

See the Work with Big Visible Charts

Maybe you've seen this scenario on a project: At 10 AM, a developer strides up to a large wall chart covered with cards arranged in columns. She moves two cards from the In Progress column to the Completed column. She looks at the cards in the In Queue column, signs her name to a card, and moves it to the In Progress column. Throughout the day, developers and testers repeat the process.

Around 3 PM, a tester walks to the task board and places a red dot on a task card in the In Progress column. At 4 PM, the team gathers round the task board. Seeing the red dot—indicating a task is in trouble—they gather information and start analyzing the problem. Two developers head off together to work on the problem.

The people on this team know what they have to do, and they do it. They don't need or want much day-to-day guidance. Their manager focuses on removing obstacles, coaching, and developing the capacity of the group.

This isn't magic. People know what to do and do it when *managers* use techniques that help people see the status of the work, planned, in progress, and completed. Big Visible Charts (BVCs) posted for all to see fit the bill.

One manager we know uses a hand-drawn matrix on a whiteboard to keep the project portfolio visible. The left-most column is the list of projects. Each of the remaining columns represents a week. For each person on his team, he has seven magnets; the magnets show which projects each person will work on in the next seven weeks.

When his manager demanded more work from his group, he walked her over to the whiteboard, and asked, "What don't you want me to do? We can unstaff anything you like to staff something else." Because the data was right there in front of her eyes, the senior manager could see she would have to make trade-offs, not just add a task.

BVCs aren't just for projects tasks and project data. We use them for workgroup trends, defect trends, defect density—anything that everyone in the group needs to see. Don't worry about having polished, computer-drawn charts; visibility is the goal, not sophisticated presentation.

ing with their director in a couple of days. We'll discuss how to collaborate on this."

Ginger covered her face with her hands. "Oh, joy," she groaned.

The group spent the next forty-five minutes arranging and rearranging sticky notes until they were satisfied they understood the earliest possible start for each person on each feature.

"Whew. Now we can review staffing," Sam said. "We've got our best people on our most important projects, right? That includes people with potential who are in assignments specifically to learn new skills."

Everyone nodded.

"Where are we understaffed?" Sam asked.

"Actually, now that I look at it this way, I think we can cover the most important work," Ginger said.

Sam nodded. "When you remove the work that's not providing business value, it's much easier to see how to accomplish the strategically important work. I'll talk with Marty about the work that needs to be done—but not by us."

"Congratulations! We've done our first version of a project portfolio. This is going to guide us for the next few weeks," Sam said.

Managing the Project Portfolio

Once you've established what work your group should be doing, lay out a plan that shows how the people in your group are going to accomplish the work.[9]

Senior management supplies strategic goals to the organization. Each layer of management below refines those strategic goals into successively more tactical goals and actions. In hierarchies, each level supports the goals of the level above.

Your job as a manager is to match the work your group does to the mission of your group and ensure it supports *your* manager's goals.

Figure 2.3: COMPLETED PROJECT PORTFOLIO

Prioritize the work. Staff the most strategically important work first. The strategic work may be the work that keeps you from fire fighting, or it may be work that directly ties to the goals. Make sure everyone knows what the priorities are and which work you want to accomplish first.

Staff the most important work. Staff less important projects after the most important ones are adequately covered. Don't staff canceled projects or the not-to-do list. Don't expect projects to limp along with inadequate staffing. Understaffed projects hinder the entire organization.

Cancel, postpone, or sequence them in a way that allows the work to proceed at a reasonable pace. Lobby for more staff when projects are truly critical and not currently staffed.

Assign people to one project at a time. Resist the urge to assign individuals to multiple projects at the same time. Multitasking may look like it allows you to accomplish more work, but it actually slows work down.[11][4] People don't multitask well because they are not machines.

Computers can swap out state, keeping a perfect copy of everything in memory. People, no matter how good their short-term memory is, are not good at swapping out a perfect copy of their state of mind. Even if they could swap out, people aren't good at swapping the same state back in.

You may have a boss who doesn't believe the data. Your boss may tell you to work overtime, suck it up, or just multitask. Don't fall for it. Trying to do it all leads to burnout.

Plan to replan. When priorities change, update the plan to reflect those changes. Revisit the plan every four to six weeks. Remove work that's complete, add new information, and add detail for the next few weeks. Also, reconfirm priorities, and adjust accordingly.

When priorities change, assignments change. The more frequently a person's assignment changes, the less work that person *completes*. When priorities change so often that nothing is ever finished, the organization has a major problem.

Now Try This

- Clarify the goals for your group. See whether you can clearly state the goal of your department. Once you can, see if your boss agrees. Once you and your boss are in agreement about key goals, ask the people in your group how *they* see the group's goals. Use this to start a discussion about how your group adds value in the organization and what they think the most important deliverables are. Make sure everyone has a clear understanding of the goal you are mutually accountable for. Review *Setting SMART Goals* on page 138 for some ideas.

- Create a first draft of the project portfolio. Clear a wall in a conference room, and using the list of work you created last week, block out the work, week by week. If you become stuck, review *Project Portfolio Planning Tips* on page 156.

- In your next series of one-on-ones, ask what people find satisfying about their work. Ask what skills they'd like to work on and whether they want to continue developing their skills in the same job. Be open to people who want to perform different work. Look for ways to support that shift within your group. If someone does want to transfer from your group, analyze the job so you can hire an appropriate replacement.

Bibliography for Chapter

[1] Lou Adler. *Hire with Your Head: Using Power Hiring to Build Great Companies.* John Wiley & Sons, Hoboken, NJ, 2002.

[2] Michael Bolton. "Are You Ready?" *STQE*, pages 50–54, May 2003.

[3] Marcus Buckingham and Curt Coffman. *First, Break All the Rules: What the World's Greatest Managers Do Differently.* Simon and Schuster, New York, NY, 1999.

[4] Tom DeMarco. *Slack: Getting Past Burnout, Busywork, and the Myth of Total Efficiency.* Broadway Books, New York, 2001.

[5] Tom Demarco and Timothy Lister. *Peopleware: Productive Projects and Teams.* Dorset House, New York, NY, second edition, 1999.

[6] Esther Derby. "Hiring for a Collaborative Team." *Computerworld.com*, April 2004. http://www.computerworld.com.

[7] Esther Derby. "Setting Clear Priorities." *Computerworld.com*, January 2004.

[8] Tom Janz, Lowell Hellerik, and David C. Gilmore. *Behavior Description Interviewing*. Prentice-Hall, Englewood Cliffs, NJ, 1986.

[9] Johanna Rothman. "Project Portfolio Management 101." *Business-IT Alignment E-Mail Advisor*, October 2001.

[10] Johanna Rothman. *Hiring the Best Knowledge Workers, Techies, and Nerds: The Secrets and Science of Hiring Technical People*. Dorset House, New York, 2004.

[11] Gerald M. Weinberg. *Quality Software Management: Volume 1, Systems Thinking*. Dorset House Publishing, Inc., New York, 1992.

Week Three
Building the Team

If you've ever worked on a jelled team, you know how good it feels. A jelled team has energy. People accomplish great feats. They celebrate and laugh together. They disagree and argue but not disagreeably. Jelled teams don't happen by accident; teams jell when someone pays attention to building trust and commitment. The jelled teams we've seen create and work toward shared goals. Over time they build trust by exchanging and honoring commitments to each other.

Teams, especially management teams, require common goals in order to work together—otherwise, they'll work as individuals. A development manager doesn't *have to* cooperate with a test manager to be successful—but the quality of the product will suffer. A test manager doesn't *have to* cooperate with other managers—but the schedule will suffer. A project manager doesn't *have to* negotiate with other project managers for scarce resources—but all the other projects will suffer. A VP of Support doesn't have to cooperate with a VP of Engineering—but customer satisfaction, product quality, and release schedules will suffer. The greater each manager's span of control in the organization, the more people are affected (negatively) by the lack of cooperation.

Individual managers will naturally optimize for their own success—often at the expense of the entire organization. But creating a management team allows the department and the individual managers to succeed.

Goals have to be real and easily recognizable as valuable. Manufactured goals aren't compelling—for instance, organizing the release

How Is a Group Different from a Team?

Is your group a team or a workgroup? It's great to be a team, but not every workgroup needs to function as a team. The difference is in six characteristics.[5]

Teams:

- are usually small—they have five to ten members.
- are committed to a common purpose or goal.
- have an agreed-upon approach to the work.
- have complementary skills.
- have interrelated or interdependent interim goals.
- make commitments about tasks to each other.

celebration doesn't support management team formation. Manufactured goals don't help people see that they need to work together for the department to succeed. Look for systemic problems that the managers need to work together to solve.

Members of a team *must* work together to succeed. Management may charter a team; the team makes their commitments to each other, not the manager. Productive and effective teams have members who know how to provide peer-to-peer feedback and navigate their way through conflict.

That doesn't mean that a workgroup—one where members may have similar skills and independent goals—can't work in a collaborative way. Workgroups share information, help each other, and sometimes make decisions together. But everyone has individual goals, not group goals.

A jelled team with shared goals can outperform a similarly skilled group working as individuals.[5] But before you decide to invest in team building, determine whether there really is a need for your group to become a team.

◇◇◇

Monday Morning

After tackling the project portfolio, Sam decided it was time to develop management team goals—goals that the entire management team would work on together. He could see that each of his managers was working hard to succeed within his or her own function—and missing opportunities to improve the overall performance of the department.

Sam sent an email announcing the first regular management team meeting.

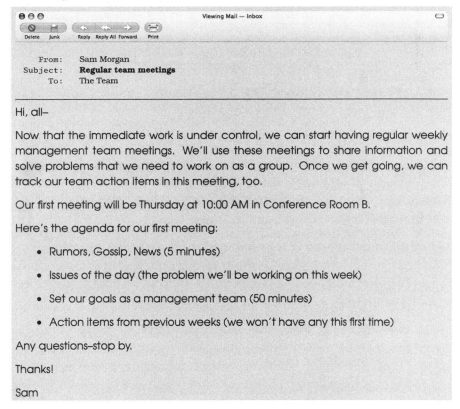

Thursday Morning

At 10:00 AM on Thursday morning, the entire crew filed into Conference Room B.

Sam sat down and pulled out his paper and pen.

"Heard any good rumors?" he asked.

Ginger and Jason chuckled.

"I hear Operations is going to hire ten more people in the next month," Jason said.

"Oh. What's the implication if that's true—what does that mean to us?" asked Sam.

"I'll have to help interview, and we do the bulk of the training," Jason responded.

"That would certainly affect the planning we did last week," Sam said. "This is ad hoc work at its best—it comes out of nowhere and affects everything. Has anyone else heard about the hiring in operations?"

"Nope, this one is new to me," Ginger proclaimed.

"Okay, I'll take that one on. Any other rumors?" asked Sam.

After a few seconds of silence, Sam asked, "Ready to continue?" Everyone nodded.

"I have some news. We have another large customer, BigCompany. They bought $5 million worth of product over the next two years," said Sam. "That means it's even more important for us to figure out how to release the product on time.

"The BigCompany news is a good lead-in for our next agenda item, setting our goals as a management team. Now that we know what we're doing for the next three to four weeks, let's shift to more strategic thinking.

"You know from last week that our department is being asked to increase revenue and decrease operations costs. We're going to have a hard time doing that unless we work together as a management team. So, I want us to define some goals for this team related to the department goal.

"Okay, let's look at where we want to be in three months.

"What are practical ways we can contribute to reducing costs and increasing revenue?" Sam handed around stacks of sticky notes and markers. "Start writing them down, one on each sticky. Then we'll group them to see what the common themes are."

After seven minutes, when he saw the pens stop moving, Sam cleared his throat. "Okay, everybody done?" Everyone nodded.

"Alright, let's start organizing these on the wall. Come up and place your stickies on the wall, and we'll cluster them as a group."

Ginger jumped from her chair and strode to the front of the room. "The number of releases," she said, slapping a sticky on the wall. "Bug fixes when Marketing changes their tiny little minds again!" She slapped another sticky on the wall.

"That affected us, too," said Patty. She placed a sticky, "ripple effects from changes in requirements" right next to Ginger's bug-fix sticky.

Kevin and Jason joined in, calling out their stickies, asking questions, and repositioning stickies. In ten minutes they had five distinct clusters.

Sam stood back and looked at the clusters. "What's the common theme in each of these clusters?" he asked.

Kevin pointed. "That one at the top is about more releases than we know how to fit into a year," said Kevin. The others nodded in agreement.

"I think the second one is about rework—working on the same features again and again until we get them right," said Jason.

"I feel like the third one is about how we use contractors," Patty said.

The group continued until they'd stated the theme for each of the clusters.

"Which of these has the biggest effect on costs and revenue?" asked Sam.

"Rework and schedule. If we can't release on time, our revenue numbers are affected. And if we have to keep fixing it, we get hit with operations and support costs," said Jason. "And the problems ripple into the next releases."

"I think you're right," said Patty. Ginger and Kevin nodded in agreement.

Now that the group had identified issues that prevented them from reaching their goals, they could define actions to change how they worked.

Figure 3.1: AFFINITY GROUPING OF IDEAS.

"Okay," said Sam. "Now I want you to do some work to identify the concrete actions we can take as a management team to release more often. Take five minutes, and write down the most important actions we can take as a team. Then we'll compare notes and build an action plan for us as a management team."

When the five minutes were up, Sam asked to hear what people had written as key actions.

"Work harder," said Patty.

"How is that different from the way you're working now?" asked Sam.

"We work hard now," said Patty. "But I guess we don't always work on the right tasks to finish a specific release."

Jason interrupted, "I know. Instead of saying 'work harder,' let's say something like 'release internally once a month.' If we're doing small internal releases of completed features and fixes, we have the option to release externally more often. Maybe when Marketing sees more working features more often, they won't try to throw everything plus the kitchen sink into every release."

"That's a great idea. How do we make 'release internally once a month' happen? What steps do we need to take? Here's an example of what I'm looking for. Say we decide that our main action is 'Update the build system so we can build every day.' Because right now, we build once a week, and that won't get us to internal releases once a month. That's a big task. Let's see if we can break this down into smaller steps. What's the first action you need to take to make that happen?" Sam asked.

Jason said, "Since I own the build system, I can update the build system. I'll start this week."

"Wait a minute," Sam said. "We're all in this together. Let's share the work. I'm sure that Ginger, Kevin, and Patty can all take steps to attain this group goal. Kevin, which steps will you take? Ginger? Patty?" The team reviewed their previous lists and translated them all into concrete steps.

UPDATE BUILD SYSTEM
(so we can build everyday)

ACTION	WHO	WHEN
ID where/why it takes so long now	Jason	MON
Make u smoke test for each component 1 a week 'til done	Ginger Patty Jason Kevin	1 a week by THURS
De-tangle by component		
– middleware	Kevin	THURS
– id how for backend	Jason	2 wks
– id issues for DB	Patty	THURS
– Uf already done? (confirm)	Ginger	THURS

Figure 3.2: ACTION PLAN FOR UPDATE BUILD SYSTEM.

By the end of the meeting, Sam's management team had a list of actions they'd take in the next week, the next month, and the following month. Taken together, the team had a plan they believed would help them reduce rework and therefore improve profits.

Creating Shared Goals

When managers don't have shared goals, they tend to optimize their own functions, often at the expense of the department's overall goals.[6] Managers who don't have shared goals fight for turf and work at cross-purposes. Creating shared goals forces the group to act as a team—or fail.[5]

Develop shared management goals as a team. Creating shared management goals as part of a regular, ongoing management team meeting reinforces that this is a normal team activity—part of how managers work together.

Facilitate shared goal development. Use brainstorming (oral or written[9]), affinity grouping, or other techniques that use everyone's input to develop the shared goals. Use techniques that incorporate the diversity of opinions and allow the group to converge on a shared goal.[4]

Develop an action plan. Goals without actions are just words. Actions have verbs and are time-bound. Create discrete, achievable steps that one person can accomplish within two weeks or less. Each team member should take responsibility for one or more actions.

Follow up on actions. Track actions against management team goals in a regular weekly management team meeting. If you don't follow up, people think the team goals are not important, and you're back where you started—with a group, not a team.

Monday Morning

Patty joined Sam in his office at 9 AM. She wasn't looking forward to this meeting—in fact, she was dreading it. This was the part of management Patty hated most. She knew she needed to talk with Amanda and Ross about their performance—and she didn't know how.

"Are you ready, Patty?" asked Sam.

"I guess so. I'm a little nervous," she said, fidgeting with her pen.

"That makes sense. You're about to do something that's not comfortable for you. And I suspect you don't have much practice giving feedback at work. And truthfully, giving effective feedback is difficult when you don't know how."

Patty and Sam discussed specific examples for both Amanda and Ross and were now ready to discuss how to have the conversation.

"First, I'll talk about the examples," said Patty.

"How are you going to do that?" Sam prompted.

"I'm going to say 'Amanda, I've observed that your last three deliverables to Jason's group were late and incomplete,' and I'll be specific about what the deliverables were, when the dates were, and how I knew they were incomplete."

"Great. That's specific. Did she know what "complete" meant when you assigned her the work? If not, she might disagree with you."

Patty furrowed her brow. "Oh, I thought I was clear. Maybe I wasn't?" Patty asked, puzzled.

"We don't know if you were or not. The point here is for you and Amanda to agree on as much data as you can and find a way to move forward."

"Okay, then I'm going to say, 'This seems to be a pattern. Many of your deliverables have been late over the last year. This isn't new behavior. This is inadequate performance.'"

Sam held up a hand. "Whoa. Slow down," said Sam, "She hasn't heard any of this before. We want to be sure to say it in a way that she can hear it now, without making her defensive. Don't call it a pattern at this point. After all, you haven't given her specific enough feedback before. Instead, why don't you say something like this: 'I've noticed that three of your deliverables have been late in the last two weeks. What can you tell me about that?'

"After all, she might have a legitimate reason, and you'll want to coach her to let you know ahead of time when she's run into a roadblock."

"I'm worried she'll get upset that I haven't said anything before now." Patty said. "She might start to cry." Patty looked like *she* might start to cry.

Failure to Give Feedback Costs More than Money

Giving feedback, especially on poor performance or touchy interpersonal issues, is hard. Preparing for a difficult feedback conversation can still make our palms sweat. But we do it anyway. Why? Because the cost of failing to provide feedback far outweighs the temporary discomfort of giving feedback. Managers who fail to give feedback lose trust and productivity. When managers fail to give feedback, problems fester and resentment builds.

Loss of trust. Surprising a team member with a long list of performance complaints at a performance review isn't helpful. Waiting weeks or months to deliver feedback leaves the team member wondering, "Why didn't he tell me? Did he want me to fail?" Timely feedback catches problems when they're small, easier to fix, and not such a big deal.

Loss of productivity. Most people want to do a good job. A manager who tells a team member that he or she needs to improve is giving the person a choice and a chance to improve. Withholding information that could help a person improve entrenches lower productivity—for that person and for the team.

Simmering resentment. People who work closely together know who is doing a good job and which team members are skating by. When managers don't do their management job—providing feedback and directly addressing performance problems—team members resent the non-performing person *and* the manager.

Providing good feedback is a necessary part of management. Preparing to give negative feedback can feel as if you're struggling with the weight of the world on your shoulders. Even giving positive feedback can be challenging.

Prepare, practice if necessary, and give the feedback anyway. In the long run, it's easier to give feedback than to let problems simmer.

"That's why we're not going to talk about the last year, we're going to talk only about recent events," said Sam. "If she does start to cry, push a box of tissues across the desk and offer her a minute to become composed. The key is to be compassionate but firm. Don't stop the meeting."

"Okay, we've got Amanda covered; what about Ross?" Patty asked.

"His situation is a little different, right?" Sam asked. "He seems to complete work on time, but it's full of defects. We need to get him to clean up his code before he submits it. So what are you going to say to Ross?"

"I'll say, 'Ross, now that Sam is here, we've been paying more attention to rework. I've noticed that your last three deliverables had more than four reported defects each.'"

"Good!" Sam nodded. "How do you think he'll react?"

"I think he'll be surprised. We've been posting the aggregate defect data for a few weeks, but I'm not sure he has looked at his individual defect data," Patty said. "My guess is he'll want to do a better job once he realizes his code is causing problems for other people."

"Excellent. Sometimes people really don't know that their work isn't up to par. Let's hope he sees that. You can monitor that during your one-on-ones with him."

"What happens if the feedback doesn't work?" Patty asked.

"If you work with both of them for a few weeks and still nothing changes, then we look at a get-well plan to bring their performance to where we need it. With a get-well plan, you'll formalize what you expect from them at work, and set up a timeline—say four to five weeks—for them to demonstrate they can achieve those expectations. I hope we won't need to do that."

"Yeah, that makes sense," Patty sighed. "I wish someone had told me this stuff a year ago when I took this job."

Provide Timely Feedback

People want to do a good job, but many people don't know what to do or how to do it. People need information to know what they're doing well and what they are doing that just isn't working.[3] Your feedback will help them tune their work.

Provide feedback as close to the event as possible. Waiting until a year-end review is not helpful.[8] Even waiting until a quarter-end or month-end is not helpful. If you wait until formal feedback opportunities, you are not giving feedback frequently enough. Providing frequent feedback prevents nasty surprises.

Deliver feedback in private. People deserve a private conversation to hear information that may be difficult or upsetting.

Describe the behavior or result. The words you choose go a long way in determining whether the other person will hear your concerns. Be descriptive both for correcting and for reinforcing feedback. "Atta boy," "atta girl," or "good job" doesn't provide any information to people about what they are doing right.

Labels don't help you make your point—they just make the other person feel bad. People are more likely to acknowledge specific data, which creates an opening for a conversation.[2] Instead of saying, "Your work is sloppy," say, "I noticed in the last set of release notes, there were typing and spelling errors."

Blanket statements beg for one exception. Instead of "You never test your code," say, "When you checked these last three changes in, the build broke each time."

Evaluations are different from feedback. Feedback is *information*. Statements like "good job" or "you've really improved" are *evaluations*. Managers do need to make evaluations, but evaluations serve a different purpose than feedback.

Listen to what the other person has to say. Check for agreement on the data. Make sure you hear any new information the other person has about the event. If the other person doesn't agree with your data, that person won't change. Ask that person how he or she sees the situation. Acknowledge that you've heard their position by paraphrasing it.

Keep notes of feedback conversations. Keep informal notes of *all* performance-related conversations. For example, retain notes of every one-on-one conversation you have with your staff. If you create a paper trail only when a problem becomes serious, you run the risk of a claim of unfair discharge. Keep a record of your efforts to improve the situation.[1]

When Feedback Doesn't Correct the Situation

Start with a verbal warning. When corrective feedback doesn't work, most companies enter a formal process with legal ramifications. Talk to your company's Human Resources department or your corporate lawyer to see how to stay within your corporate guidelines and the law.

When corrective feedback isn't working, make sure your employee knows the situation is serious. Verbal warnings need to be clear and unambiguous: "This [instance of work] is unacceptable as a deliverable [state specific reasons]. We've talked about this issue before. This is a verbal warning that you have to change your work if you want to keep your job."

Deliver a written warning. When a verbal warning doesn't produce change and your company requires a written warning, repeat the warning in writing. Include dates and times of previous conversations related to poor performance.

Implement a get-well plan. Along with the verbal or written warning, implement a get-well plan. A get-well plan is a short period (four to five weeks) where the employee must show evidence that he is meeting acceptable standards. If at any time the employee's work doesn't meet the standard, terminate the plan and terminate employment.[7]

Don't underestimate the impact of poor performance. Anyone can have a bad day once in a while. But long-term poor performance affects not only the results but the morale of the entire team. If poor performance is ongoing, discuss and resolve those issues.

Now Try This

- Assess your group meetings. Are your meetings providing a relevant exchange of information between all the participants? Do your meetings have action-oriented outcomes? Use the guidelines in *Run Effective Meetings* on page 143 to improve your meetings. Review the section on page 148 if you're not sure what to use as an agenda.

- Provide feedback to each person during one-on-one meetings. Give feedback on something that's going well. If you see a problem, use the one-on-one to provide information on what needs to change.

- Ask yourself whether you've been deliberately avoiding any feedback issues. If so, what's preventing you from providing feedback? See *Guide to Giving Effective Feedback* on page 134 to troubleshoot your feedback problems.

Bibliography for Chapter

[1] Tom Coens and Mary Jenkins. *Abolishing Performance Appraisals: Why They Backfire and What to Do Instead.* Barrertt-Koehler, San Francisco, 2002.

[2] Esther Derby. "How to Talk About Work Performance: A Feedback Primer." *Crosstalk*, pages 13–16, December 2003.

[3] Ferdinand F. Fournies. *Coaching for Improved Work Performance.* McGraw Hill, New York, 2000.

[4] Sam Kaner. *The Facilitator's Guide to Participatory Decision-Making.* New Society Publishers, Gabriola Island, BC, 1996.

[5] Jon R. Katzenbach and Douglas K. Smith. *The Wisdom of Team: Creating the High-Performance Organization.* Harper-Collins Publishers, New York, 1999.

[6] Patrick Lencioni. *The Five Dysfunctions of a Team: A Leadership Fable.* Jossey-Bass, A Wiley Company, San Francisco, 2002.

[7] Johanna Rothman. "Successful Software Management: Fourteen Lessons Learned." *Crosstalk*, pages 17–20, December 2003.

[8] Charles Seashore, Edith Seashore, and Gerald M. Weinberg. *What Did You Say? The Art of Giving and Receiving Feedback.* Bingham House Books, Columbia, MD, 1997.

[9] Brian R. Stanfield. *The Workshop Book: From Individual Creativity to Group Action (Ica Series).* New Society Publishing, Gabriola Island, BC, 2002.

Week Four
Managing Day by Day

Each person on your team is unique. Some will need feedback on personal behaviors. Some will need help defining career development goals. Some will need coaching on how to influence across the organization.

Individual coaching, day by day, is how you build people's capacity, your relationships with them, and trust between the two of you. Let's look at how Sam does it.

Monday

As Kevin headed to Sam's office for his one-on-one, he reflected: *I thought these one-on-ones would be a waste of time, but they're not. I have a bunch of topics to review with Sam today.*

"Hi, Kevin. How's it going?" asked Sam.

Kevin straightened up in his chair. "We're making progress. We finished one of the four features. Turns out that keeping people on one feature at a time was a good idea. We finished feature A in less time than I'd expected. We still have three more features to do. It's going to be a challenge to finish them on time."

"Which one is next?" Sam asked.

"Feature B is next in line," Kevin answered.

Kevin and Sam finished reviewing progress and action items.

Who's Responsible for Career Development?

The short answer is that both the manager and the staffer are responsible. Both people have the role of considering the staff person's strengths, aptitudes, and interests. Together, they discuss career development and develop action plans.

It doesn't matter who initiates the conversation, as long as someone does. Here's what does matter:

- The manager initiates the career development in one-on-ones periodically. We recommend quarterly.
- Both people verify the career development goals are still valid.
- Both people monitor progress against goals.
- The manager looks for opportunities to advance the team member's career.

Make sure the career development plans are integrated into the person's day-to-day work. Otherwise, career development won't happen.

Sam asked, "Last week we talked about developing your goals for the next few months—the skills and techniques you want to learn that will help you do your job better. Are you ready to start talking about that?"

"I thought we did that last week in our management team meeting," Kevin said.

"Those were our management team goals. You're responsible for some of the actions that accomplish the team goal. But now I'm talking about individual goals—specific skills you want to improve."

"Oh, I see," Kevin said. "I'd like to learn more about project management. I think I could use more project management techniques to organize our work."

"That's a great goal," said Sam. "Becoming a great project manager is a long-term endeavor, but you can start with small steps and have those as your individual goals."

Sam and Kevin discussed the first steps to become a better project manager and developed an action plan for Kevin's goal. Kevin's action plan looked like this:

1. Within the next month, learn more about project scoping and project charters by reading articles and books related to starting projects.

2. Work with the management team to write a project charter for the next release.

3. Within the next month, read articles about iterative incremental development. Present findings to the management team, and lead the group in a discussion on how to deliver features more effectively.

4. Identify my biggest challenge in organizing my work.

"That's all I need to do?" Kevin asked.

"For now," Sam replied. "Next month, you'll take a few more small steps to build more skills. We're going to build your project management skills step by step, practicing along the way."

Create Individual Goals for Each Person

Goals don't have to address the entire year. In fact, it's more effective to have a series of short-term goals that build incrementally to what you want to achieve.[5]

Provide context with corporate and department missions and goals. People need context in order to select reasonable goals for themselves.[9] Without the context, it's easy to focus on personal interests and preferences at the expense of the organization's needs.

Establish individual goals. Work collaboratively to establish goals with each individual. Each person needs his or her own individual goals. Individual goals can address problems, or they can address work-related skills. Decompose the goals into action items. Without an action plan, goals remain high-level and unattainable. People achieve goals by establishing clear steps to reach the end, not by merely noting the desired end. When you invest your time working with individuals on *their* goals, you communicate that you care about their development.

Create small steps for action plans. People don't accomplish goals in one giant leap. People reach goals one small step at a time. Huge steps are put off until tomorrow; small steps are achievable today. If you learn new skills in small steps, incorporating practice with feedback, it's easier to learn and succeed. [3][8][7]

Track action plans in one-on-one meetings. As with group goals, tracking actions communicates that the goal is important. If you never ask again, you communicate that goals and action plans are unimportant.

Monday Midmorning

Jason was stumped. He knew Sam wanted to reduce the time the Backend group spent supporting the Operations group. And he wanted to move training over to Operations. But he wasn't sure how. Jason frowned as he entered Sam's office for his one-on-one.

"Sam, I understand you want to reduce our Operations support time, and training is a big part of that." Jason said. "If I just drop the training, all hell will break loose, and the situation will actually become worse."

"You're right," agreed Sam. "We have to find a way to transition the training out of your group and into Operations where it belongs. How did you come to have responsibility for the training?"

"I know it doesn't look like it makes sense now, but it did at one time. My group used to *be* Operations. When Operations became a separate group, the old director promoted Clyde from my group. Clyde is a great guy—but he doesn't plan ahead. I took over training in self-defense. If I don't train the Ops guys, they don't get trained."

"I can see where those decisions made sense at the time," Sam said. "It was the right thing to do to make sure Operations had the information they needed about new releases. It seems to me that the company is in a different place now. It's a good time to reexamine where the training function really belongs.

"What options have you considered to move training out of your group?" Sam asked.

"I thought about meeting with Clyde to tell him he has to do the training," Jason said. "But I don't see how anything will be different with Clyde now than it was before. I can't just drop it; that's too painful for my group. You could talk to Clyde's boss—that might work."

"Yeah, that might work, but maybe we can come up with some other options," said Sam. "Is the training for new hires written down?"

"Part of it is. But some stuff changes with every release," Jason replied.

"Do you write down the release changes?"

"Some of it," Jason said. "We write down a lot of it, but as we make improvements and fixes, it changes, and we don't always keep up."

"The fact that some of it's written down means that we could do a train-the-trainer in Clyde's group for a lot of the new hire training. So, maybe we can eliminate 75% of the new hire training?"

"That sounds about right," Jason said.

"How much time would that buy you?" asked Sam.

"We'd save about twelve hours every time they add someone new. We'd still spend about four hours, but maybe we could batch it and train the new hires in groups."

"Could anyone else do the training aside from someone in Clyde's group?" Sam asked.

"Actually, the tech writer who wrote the last release notes asked how we were going to train the Ops staff, and he made some really good suggestions. Maybe he could do it."

"Sounds like we have several options now: you talk to Clyde, I talk to Clyde's boss, you approach Clyde about trying train-the-trainer, or we talk to the Tech Pubs manager about having his guy take over the training," Sam said.

"I think I should talk to Clyde first about doing train-the-trainer," Jason said. "He might go for that."

"Let's make that one of your action items. Next week we'll talk more about moving the release training off your plate."

Coaching for Success

Coaching helps your staff become better problem-solvers, learn new skills, and meet their goals.

Spend time coaching when it's worth your time to do so—when the risk of your employee failing in this part of their role is too high—or when they ask for help.[7][4] People may not be aware that they are stuck or that their work is at risk—that's the time to coach.

Coaching is a kind of helping. Coaching doesn't mean you rush in to solve the problem. Coaching helps the other person see more options and choose from them. Coaching helps another person develop new capability with support.

Generate options. Our rule of thumb is to generate at least three reasonable options for solving any problem (see the sidebar on the next page). Generating three options breaks the logjam. Rather than offer options on a silver plate, collaboratively generate and discuss options with the employee.[7]

Walk through implications. Jointly review the implications of various options to help choose the most appropriate one. Helping someone think through the implications is the meat of coaching.

Develop an action plan. Outline the first steps necessary to take action. Options without actions don't happen.

Follow up on progress during one-on-ones. One-on-ones provide you the perfect opportunity to ask about progress, provide support, and ask whether more help is wanted.

Coaching goes only so far. When you find yourself coaching someone about the same issues over and over, decide whether the person has the ability to learn from your coaching. The failure may be due to your coaching or the other person's abilities. You may be missing an underlying issue. It's also possible that the person is in the wrong job.

Rule of Three

People are great problem-solvers—except when they're not. When people aren't being great problem-solvers, they tend to latch onto the first plausible alternative. Sometimes the first alternative is the best solution. More often, the best solution is the third, fourth, or fifth possibility.

The Rule of Three[10] is a guideline for making better decisions. Here's how it goes:

One alternative is a trap. There's only one solution, and if it doesn't work, you're out of luck and out of options.

Two alternatives is a dilemma. Two alternatives is false choice: there's only *this* or *that*.

Three alternatives provide a real choice. With three alternatives you can make a real choice.

Once people come up with the third alternative, it's easy to come up with several more. We've used the Rule of Three for the following:

- Evaluating alternatives for organizing projects
- Considering how to structure work and organize technical staff, technical leads, and managers so that everyone can work effectively
- Generating system architectures and designs
- Brainstorming what could go wrong with a design or architecture
- Brainstorming risks that could prevent a project from moving forward
- Evaluating desirable outcomes
- Considering other possible interpretations for someone else's statement or behavior

(continued...)

If you believe someone needs coaching to be successful, and he or she isn't interested, don't coach. Move into corrective feedback and possibly a get-well plan.[7]

Here are some guidelines for applying the Rule of Three:

- Keep an open mind about who will implement the alternatives. First generate the alternatives. Then worry about who will carry out the options.
- Consider alternatives even if you don't know *how* you'll accomplish them. The *how* comes later.
- Generate worthy alternatives. Simply listing one good option and two bozo options doesn't count. All the alternatives must be worthy of serious consideration, even if you don't *like* them.
- Disqualify an alternative only after evaluation.
- Be open to hybrid solutions. Once you start analyzing alternatives, you may see that combining features of one or more options will work best.

Even if you do choose the first option, you'll understand the issue better after considering several options.

Later That Same Day

On his way back from lunch, Jason ran into Clyde. Jason decided to take advantage of the moment and broach the training issue. Clyde was not receptive.

Jason emailed Sam to ask for help.

Sam read Jason's email and thought, *Uh oh. Sound like Jason might have used the wrong approach. Still, Jason has to transition training back to Clyde. I'll stop by and see where I can help.* Sam headed for Jason's office.

Sam poked his head into Jason's office. "You want to talk about your conversation with Clyde?"

"It didn't go well. He doesn't want responsibility for the training. He says he doesn't have enough time or people to do the training himself. Now what? Are you going to talk to his boss?"

"Let's review what happened, and then we'll talk about next steps."

Jason recapped the conversation for Sam. Sam said, "Let's see if you can't address this again with Clyde before I have to get involved. If I go over Clyde's head, it may make your working relationship with him more difficult."

A look of understanding crossed Jason's face. "I see your point. What else can I say to Clyde?"

"First, let's look at it from Clyde's point of view. What does he lose by taking on the training?"

"He told me he loses time—time he thinks he needs to use for the Operations work." Jason thought for a while. "I feel bad saying this, but he also loses the ability to blame me if his guys aren't trained well."

"You may be right. He may also be afraid that he doesn't know how to organize the material or deliver the training."

"What do you think he'll gain?"

"He gets to train his guys the way he wants, when he wants, and he has control over the material. He's less dependent on my group and me, which may be a downside for me. We've been using the training to help the groups get to know each other. I'm not sure what we'll do now."

"Can we make a case with Clyde about what he wins and address his concerns about what he loses?" Sam thought for a minute, tapping his fingers against his chin. "Given your relationship with Clyde, maybe it makes more sense for you to approach this as a joint problem. You and he could sit down and discuss what each of you wins and loses—and then decide what's best for the company in the long run."

Jason replied, "I like the idea of sitting down with him to discuss what's right for the company."

Learning to Influence

In most organizations, we can't accomplish much on our own. This is especially true for managers. To accomplish our work, we work

I'll Scratch Your Back If You Scratch Mine

Imagine this scene: You've realized that the urgent project you're attempting to staff reaches across your group into several other groups. Of course, your peer managers don't feel the same urgency for this project that you do. How will you get them to help you accomplish this work? This is where influence and negotiation come into play.

Emphasize mutual benefit. Engage their support by showing them that participating in your urgent project will benefit *them*, not just you.

Appeal to greater goals. Explain how the results of the project will affect company goals and revenues. Enlist support by emphasizing the greater good. Be willing to share credit with all the other people who help you achieve the project goals.

Horse trade. Maybe you are in a position to help another manager with an issue she is facing. You may have machines, lab time, skills, or some other resource that she needs. Offer a straight-up trade.

Reciprocate. Next time around, you may be the one who has resources to help someone else. Managers who only ask for help and never reciprocate end up losing influence and support.

Managers are often measured and rewarded for what appears to be "their" group's work. But much of the time, a single manager just can't be successful working alone. Cultivate relationships with peers in advance so you can influence and negotiate when you need help.

with other people across the organization to find mutually beneficial solutions. This means being effective at influencing others.

Prepare for the influence conversation. Before you talk to the other person, consider what you know about the situation, from your perspective and the other's perspective.

- Describe your current context. How do you see it, and how does the other person see it?

- Identify what you want to change. How will the change benefit you, the other person, and the organization?[2]

- Identify what you and the other person could lose as a result of the change you desire.

When you ask for help, you may feel off balance or insecure, and these feelings can bleed into the conversation. Remember that none of us can be successful in organizations without the help and cooperation of others.

Discuss interests, not positions. You may have a particular solution in mind. Rather than start with that solution, begin with what you both may gain by resolving the situation. A solution represents a *position*; your aim—what you want to accomplish—speaks to your *interests* in the matter.[6] Find common ground[2] so you can discuss your interests. It works the other way, too. Discussing interests can help identify common ground.

Be ready to discover a solution together. As you discuss the issue, you may discover new solutions, solutions that solve the problem in a way that fits for both of you.

Monday Afternoon

Ginger plunked herself down across the desk from Sam. "Alright, I'm ready for our weekly therapy session."

Sam smiled. "What's going on, Ginger?"

Ginger started rattling off the work in her group. "Those idiots in Marketing. Do you know what they want to do now?" Ginger rolled her eyes.

"Hold on a second, Ginger," Sam interrupted. "Do you think they are literally idiots?"

"They irritate me. They don't understand the impact of what they are asking us to do."

"Have you ever told them?" asked Sam.

"They should know."

"People don't know unless you tell them. Let me give you a little feedback right now, so you can understand what I'm seeing."

Ginger looked startled. "What do you mean?" she asked, leaning back in her chair.

"When I hear you refer to colleagues in other departments as idiots, I wonder how it affects your ability to work with them."

"I'm just letting off steam."

"That may be so. I don't know if I'm the only person who has heard you speak this way. If your group hears you speak this way, they may think it's acceptable for them to speak and feel this way. On a practical level, it's really difficult to have a strong working relationship with someone you don't respect. And your language says you don't respect them."

"I'd never thought of it that way," Ginger said. "But what should I do? I'm frustrated with Marketing, and I need a way to blow off steam."

"I'd like you to use different language. Think like they do: what would have to be true for the Marketing people to act this way, giving you lots of changes all the time?"

Ginger thought for a moment. She tugged on her ponytail.

"Maybe the customers are telling them different things, or maybe they don't have a way to decide what it is they want. Or maybe they can't tell what they want until we actually deliver something."

"What you're saying is, it's not necessarily that they can't keep their minds set, as much as they need to see something before they understand what they want. Is that right?" Sam said.

Ginger leaned further back in her chair. "Yeah. Maybe they aren't idiots. Maybe I could show them something earlier so they don't make as many late changes."

Functioning as a Human Pressure Valve

Sometimes it helps to vent—but not at a customer, co-worker, senior manager, or someone from another department.

When someone on your team is frustrated or upset, be willing to listen. Act as a pressure valve, allowing pent-up emotion to dissipate without harm.

Acknowledge emotions verbally by saying something like "I hear you are angry about what happened." Empathize without agreeing with labels, judgments, or interpretations.

Sometimes "venting" is enough, and the team member will take appropriate action. When that doesn't happen naturally, redirect the conversation to generating constructive outcomes.

Model a process for managing strong emotions: Ask about specific facts and interpretations. Ask what a positive outcome would look like. Clarify that it's not helpful to share a label or judgment—or vent—with other people in the organization.

When venting becomes a pattern (holding grudges or obsessing about a person or incident), it's a sign of a different problem. Offer feedback and coaching about the effects of the pattern, and if necessary, suggest professional counseling.

"Maybe. The problem is you're seeing the symptoms, not the root problem. If you think of them as your colleagues, and try to imagine their point of view, you'll have a different perspective."

"I suppose so. Maybe I need to go to Charm School," she grinned.

"No, you don't need Charm School," he grinned back. "But you do need to think about how your words sound to other people. And consider how your language affects your perspective and your ability to do your job.

"What are three ways you can anticipate you are about to use derogatory labels?"

Ginger paused. "What if I notice when I'm starting to be irritated?

Flipping the Bozo Bit

Imagine this scene: One of your colleagues—we'll call him Cyril—just doesn't get it. He's sort of annoying and clueless. He has started talking about the product design again, and you've tuned him out. *Here he goes again. Why doesn't he just shut up?* you say to yourself with gritted teeth and start thinking about the soccer tournament.

You've flipped the bozo bit on Cyril—because only a clown would talk this way.

Hold on.

Cyril may not understand the issues as well as you do. But before you lose patience and assume Cyril is a bozo, ask yourself, "Do I want to work with or influence Cyril?" When we write someone off and disregard all input from that person as suspect, we diminish our ability to cooperate, work with, or influence that person. One way or another, contempt will leak through and color the working relationship.

Instead of flipping the bozo bit, make a generous interpretation of the other person's behavior, and ask this question: "Assuming that this person is smart, well-intentioned, and has legitimate motives, what would have to be true for this person to say this or act this way?"

Come up with three plausible alternatives. Because no matter how it looks, everyone is trying to be helpful[11]—even someone who may act or sound like a bozo from time to time.

Now that I think about it, I start tapping my pencil when I get frustrated. I'll listen for my pencil tapping." Ginger identified two more signs to help her notice when her irritation threatened to leak into her language.

Sam wrapped up the meeting. "Next week let me know how you're doing with monitoring your language and finding a different way to blow off steam."

◇◇◇

Capitalizing on Feedback Opportunities

People need information to learn about how well they are doing their job, both technical and interpersonal aspects. Don't surprise people at year-end. Effective feedback occurs as soon after the event as possible.[1] This is especially true for feedback about a person's behavior. People forget what they did within moments. Mention issues when they're small rather than waiting for a disaster.

If the behavior occurs in a public setting, take the person aside or use the first private moment to deliver the feedback. When behavior affects the safety of the group, give feedback immediately. Do not wait for a private moment.

Now Try This

- Look for opportunities in your one-on-ones to work with each person to improve their capabilities. Define career goals once a quarter or so; discuss progress toward career goals every week.

- List the people you work with. Now make a separate list of the people on whom your success depends. Wherever the list does *not* overlap is an opportunity to build a relationship, before you desperately need it. *Preparing for Influence* on page 153 may help you get started.

- Check your blind spots. Are you using gestures or language that reduce your effectiveness? You may want to ask a trusted colleague for help. Eliminate any demeaning or degrading language. Try stating how you feel, rather than acting it out.

Bibliography for Chapter

[1] Robert R. Blake and Jane Srygley Mouton. *The Versatile Manager: A Grid Profile.* Dow Jones-Irwin, Homewood, IL, 1980.

[2] Allen R. Cohen and David L. Bradford. *Influence without Authority.* John Wiley & Sons, New York, 1991.

[3] Esther Derby. "Climbing the Learning Curve: Practice with Feedback." *Insights*, 2002. Fall.

[4] Esther Derby. "Managing a Struggling Employee." *Insights*, 2003.

[5] Daniel Feldman. *The Manager's Pocket Guide to Workplace Coaching*. HRD Press, Amherst, MA, 2001.

[6] Roger Fisher, William Ury, and Bruce Patton. *Getting to Yes, Second ed.* Penguin Books, New York, 1991.

[7] Ferdinand F. Fournies. *Coaching for Improved Work Performance*. McGraw Hill, New York, 2000.

[8] Johanna Rothman. "Practice, a Necessary Part of Change." *Cutter IT Email Advisorory*, February 2002.

[9] Johanna Rothman. "Successful Software Management: Fourteen Lessons Learned." *Crosstalk*, pages 17–20, December 2003.

[10] Gerald M. Weinberg. *The Secrets of Consulting*. Dorset House, New York, 1985.

[11] Gerald M. Weinberg. *Becoming a Technical Leader: An Organic Problem-Solving Approach*. Dorset House, New York, 1986.

Week Five
Discovering Lurking Problems

Not every problem is an individual problem. Some problems are part of a system and can be solved only by a group of people. That system could be the development team or the testing team or a project team or a management team—or it could be even bigger and involve large portions of the organization.

A seasoned manager may be able to see the system clearly. But many people—because they are part of the system—cannot clearly see the problems or how to fix them. If you're in a position to know a problem exists, consider this guideline for problem solving: the people who perform the work need to be part of the solution.

As a manager, you may need to facilitate their problem-solving work. Or, you may need to lead those people in problem solving. But if the problem spans groups, you may need to work with your peers to solve problems as part of a management team.

Kevin slumped down in the chair across from Sam's desk and rubbed his eyes. He stifled a yawn.

"How's it going?" Sam asked.

"I'm working really hard to keep up. Middleware is always in the middle," Kevin smiled at his own joke. "Every time I think I have a handle on the work from the UI group, we get more things to do. My to-do list gets longer and longer. Ginger is pushing for this UI work, so I have to assign people."

Sustainable Pace

You've seen them: managers and technical staff who drag themselves into work every day. They stare blankly at their computer screens, yawning over an extra tall cuppa java. They're on a short fuse, and they make stupid mistakes. Sometimes their decisions are not just suspect, they appear downright wrong.

These aren't stupid people; they aren't bad people either. They're *burnt-out* people.

Whatever the manifestation, burnout occurs when there is too much to do, not enough time to do it, and the person (technical contributor or manager) attempts to do all the work anyway. Burnout, especially on the part of a manager, can take down an entire team.

The way to avoid burnout is to work on one thing at a time—eliminate multitasking—and to work at a sustainable pace.

Most people can work about 40-45 hours per week as a *sustainable* pace. Yes, it's possible to work more than 40 hours per week *for a week or two*. But any longer than that and you court burnout, mistakes, and lower productivity.[10]

This isn't news. As far back as 1909, researchers noticed that people who worked more than 40 hours a week had lower productivity.[2]

Working at a sustainable pace of 40 hours a week isn't molly-coddling. It's a smart business decision, and it's your job to make it happen.

Sam looked at Kevin and saw his eyes were red. Kevin looked bone tired. *Forget our usual one-on-one agenda. I need to find out what's going on with Kevin.* "Tell me about all this work coming from Ginger. Is the work all coming from Ginger? Is it Ginger directly? Ginger mostly?"

"It's Ginger mostly, and indirectly. Marketing comes to Ginger, Ginger comes to me," Kevin answered.

"Why does Marketing go to Ginger?" Sam asked.

"Marketing thinks they're just asking for UI changes, but it turns out that the changes have a ripple effect. My changes require internal design changes, so they're not easy or fast to make. Jason says there's backend design changes, too."

Sam asked, "How do you decide which changes to make, and when to make them?"

Kevin looked puzzled. "We just take them as they come."

"Are all the changes equally important?"

"No, of course not." Kevin shook his head and frowned. "But I can't predict when an important change is going to come in, and I have a huge backlog of work to complete now. So, when we receive something important, I juggle people's priorities and work."

"Sometimes that juggling act is difficult, eh? Is that why you have everyone working on four or five different projects at the same time?"

"Yeah. But I don't see how to fix this."

"I'm not sure yet either. What if you could plan your work? Would you assign people any differently?"

"How can I create a plan when I don't know what's coming in next week? I've been trying to make the portfolio planning work, but it's not working for me."

Sam suggested, "How about if you just plan for two weeks at a time?"

"I could plan the next couple of weeks. I don't know how to plan past that because the work changes too much." Kevin thought for a minute. "Planning for a month works only if I don't have to take changes every couple of days."

> ### Is Priority Business or Technical?
>
> Prioritizing features within a project or release is a business decision, not a technical decision.
>
> Deciding which defects to fix and when is also a business decision, *based on business impact*. A crash defect in a seldom-used module may not be as important—from a business perspective—as a lower-severity bug in a module used by thousands of customers.
>
> We use cross-functional teams—composed of developers, testers, product managers, support people, and anyone who has a stake in the outcome—to establish defect priorities. Technical people provide the background on the technical impact of the defect and the approximate schedule to fix it. (We've worked with teams that categorized defects as "easy," "moderate," and "hard" to fix.) Business people determine the business impact and determine whether it's a defect they can live with (for now).

"How do we queue our work now?" Sam asked.

"Marketing asks Ginger. Ginger tells me what she is doing. I figure out what we have to do and assign it to my group. When Patty or Jason needs to be involved, I tell them."

"This is a problem we have to work on as a management team. It's bigger than your group or any one group. I'll make this the main focus of our next group meeting." Sam said.

Kevin looked relieved. "I can't wait for the next group meeting."

Recognize Messy Problems: Problems That Are Bigger Than One Manager Can Fix

Sometimes a problem that seems like it's coming from one person is actually a problem with the process. When you aren't getting the results you want, it's time to change the processes ("the way we do things around here"). When a process problem spans more than one area, the group needs to work on it together.[7]

To detect whether it's bigger than one area do the following:

Look for artificial constraints. People often have a limited view of a situation, not because they have limited intelligence but because humans place artificial constraints on solutions. We often assume that deadlines are immutable, that a process is unchangeable, or that we have to solve something alone. Use thought experiments to remove artificial constraints, for example, "What if you don't have to predict?" Removing artificial constraints allows people to think about the problem in a different way.

Listen for pointers to the underlying problem. The problem you see may not be the one you need to solve. Consider root cause analysis to identify deeper problems.[6] System problems confound root cause analysis because many factors are interrelated. When the root cause points to the original issue, it's likely a system problem.

Look for solutions that you can implement. When the problem spans an area larger than your sphere of control, see whether you can bring in the others to solve the problem. But don't rely on them to fix the situation. Determine what you can do within your sphere of control and influence.

Fix the problem, don't affix blame. "Things are the way they are because they got that way,"[9] so it makes no sense to blame others.[1] Acknowledge that people arrived here with the best of intentions. Decisions that seem strange now made perfect sense at a different time. Trying to find a culprit may be satisfying in the short term, but doesn't help solve the problem.

Friday Morning

Sam watched as the managers entered the conference room for their weekly management team meeting and found seats around the table. He could tell from both their joking and serious discussions that they respected and trusted each other more than they had when he first met them. Flip charts covered the conference room walls. The flip charts showed action items and completed tasks for the project to fix the build system. Sam sensed that the management team was starting to jell. They were ready to start solving problems as a group in their management team meeting.

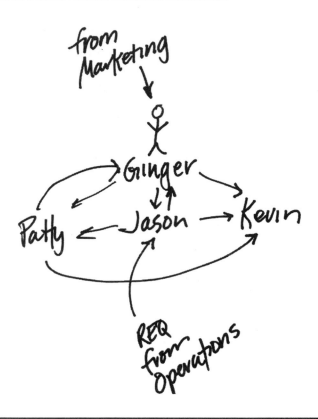

Figure 5.1: How requests enter the group.

"Okay, let's work on our issue for this week: how we manage requests. Kevin, since you brought it up, tell us how the current practice affects you."

"Okay. Ginger, you receive a bazillion requests from Marketing for changes."

Ginger nodded.

"Those changes may start out looking like GUI changes, but they end up affecting the middleware and the backend components, too," Kevin explained.

"What I'm realizing is that none of us understand the ripple effects of the changes that come into Ginger's group," Kevin said. "Ginger gets a work request, and we need to know how that change affects all of us—how big the change is, and what each of us has to do to make the change work, before we start designing or coding. We're not always working on the most important thing—at least my group isn't. When something more important comes up, we drop what we're doing and shift to that, or we add more tasks."

"Nice summary, Kevin. Thank you," said Sam. "Let's gather a little data. How do the requests come in now?"

Together they created a picture of how requests came into the group. They discovered that while Ginger thought all the changes came in through her, it turned out Patty received requests for field changes that she then handed off to Ginger and Kevin. Jason sometimes received requests from Operations that he handed off to Kevin, Ginger, and Patty.

Kevin looked at the picture and sighed. "I thought more of them came in through Ginger. This is a bigger problem than I thought."

Ginger started to say, "Those little. . . ," but clapped her hand over her mouth. "Oops. Sorry. I'm working on my language."

"I know it would be easy to push this off on Marketing," Sam said. "But before we ask them to fix the problem, let's see what we can do within our own department. Let's see if we can change the way we work before we ask someone else to change.

"This is a group problem; it affects all of us. Everyone is a source of requests. All of you would like to plan your work better. How can we channel all these requests so that we can assess their importance and how the work affects each group?"

Ginger held up her hand with all five fingers extended. "We could limit Marketing to five requests a month," Ginger offered.

"Or we could have them list everything they want to change at the beginning of the year and then sign off on it," Kevin suggested. "We'd have to let them change their minds every month, I guess."

"I could really live with changes only once a month," Jason said. "Let's do that."

"Before we decide on that, let's see if we can come up with at least one more idea so we have three to choose from," said Sam.

"We could set up a database of requests," Patty suggested. "Maybe we could start with a spreadsheet. Anyone can enter a request, but then we have to prioritize it as a group."

"That's a good idea, too," Jason said.

"So far all our ideas are about how we take in requests. What about some ideas about how we implement requests?" Sam suggested.

"We may need to do that too, but first we have to manage the flow before I have time to figure out how to develop differently," Kevin said.

Wow, thought Sam. *He's not sucking it up anymore. Good for him!* "Okay, let's return to managing the requests. Which is our best option?"

"The database," Kevin stated with conviction. "What do you guys think?"

Jason and Patty agreed. "I still want them to have only five requests a month," Ginger acceded, "but I guess I'll go along."

"So, how do we make this work? We understand the priority from our perspective. I think we need to talk to Marketing, so we understand what they need." Sam suggested.

"We need Operations, too," Jason added.

"True enough. Sounds like we need a cross-functional group to assess priority," Sam said. "What information does that group need to make good decisions?"

"They need to know if it's hard or easy to do," Ginger proposed.

"Hard or easy might be one way to categorize it," Sam agreed. "Do we know how long an easy request takes? Or a difficult one?"

"We need to know how much it will cost to support," Jason offered.

"Good. What else?"

When no one offered suggestions, Sam prompted, "How about the benefit vs. the cost to implement and how it fits with the goal for the product?"

Everyone nodded.

"Anything else we missed?"

They all shook their heads. "But we'll never squeeze all that information out of them," Patty said.

Focus, Focus, Focus

You've met those busy, busy, busy people. They run around all day, attempting to do everything. In reality, they're not accomplishing much—if anything.[4]

When we set priorities, we don't have to do everything at once, or even attempt to do everything possible. Prioritizing and sequencing work is essential to staffing work appropriately. Even more important, prioritizing focuses us on doing the work that will deliver the highest value to the company.

Defining and managing the project portfolio is difficult. And it's necessary to ensure that essential and strategically important work takes precedence and that people are working at a sustainable pace.

Sam continued. "You're right. That's asking a lot. Maybe all that information is our ultimate goal. We can start by understanding the size of the request and whether Marketing still wants it once they realize the cost to implement and support it."

"We need to discuss how often to evaluate the list and when to change priorities of our work," Sam said.

Ginger said slowly, "What if we changed our work every couple of months? Do you think that's often enough?"

Kevin replied, "Not for me. The changes come in too fast for me to try to plan a couple of months out. How about a couple of weeks?"

"Most of our requests take longer than a couple of weeks. But we can do most of them within three to four weeks. How about if we evaluate the list and change our work once a month?" Jason asked. Kevin looked skeptical, but agreed.

Patty nodded. Ginger said, "I think it's hard to break them of the habit of asking for features whenever they want, but I think it's worth a try."

Sam summarized, "It's not just their habit; it's our habit too. We're going to have to say what *easy* or *hard* means so they have enough information to make good decisions. And, we'll have to finish the work when we say we will. We'll have to back our people up to make sure that all changes go through our database of requests, not sliding in through the back door. I'll take the lead on talking to Marketing to make sure this solution meets their needs, too."

Together, the management team developed an action plan, signed up for tasks, and agreed to check in at the next management team meeting.

Solving Problems as a Management Team

Groups become teams when they realize they are interdependent, trust each other, and have shared goals. Mobilizing a team to solve problems together increases the probability of a good solution and ensures the team will own the solution.

Engage group creativity. Prescribing solutions does not work, but engaging the creativity of a team almost always results in a better solution—and one that the team will own.[3]

Describe the problem. Start by describing what the issue is and how it affects members of the group to create a shared understanding of the problem.[6]

Collect data. Before you jump to solutions, collect some data. Data collection doesn't have to be formal. Look for quantitative and qualitative data.

Write it down. Don't rely on memory and recall; write down the data you gather. Draw a picture or create a table to help people see the data. Make the data visible—use a flip chart or whiteboard—don't worry about making the data pretty or archival.

Brainstorm possible solutions. It's tempting to stop with the first reasonable option that pops into your head. But with any messy problem, generating multiple options leads to a richer understanding of the problem and potential solutions[8] (see the sidebar on page 71).

Document the decision. Make sure the decision is recorded so you can follow it consistently in the future. Revisit the decision if you need to, but do it because you wanted to revisit the decision, not because no one could remember what the group decided.

Look for areas where you can act. Even when a full solution involves areas outside your control, don't rely on others to start working on the issue. Look for areas where you can act within your own department.[5]

Develop an action plan. People don't implement solutions that don't have action plans. Plan the necessary steps, assign people and target dates to each step, and track progress.

Now Try This

- Make a list of your group's problems. Identify any that can be solved within your group, and choose one of them as the topic for your next group meeting. The problems you can't solve alone are candidates to work on with your management peers. Try using the Rule of Three on page 71 and *Solving Problems: Create New Situations* on page 154 to structure your problem-solving work.

- Stretch your group problem-solving skills. Try the techniques listed in *Facilitation Essentials for Managers* on page 128 to engage the entire group in solving problems.

- If you haven't updated the project portfolio in a couple of weeks, do it now. An out-of-date project portfolio is a useless project portfolio.

Bibliography for Chapter

[1] Mary Albright and Clay Carr. *101 Biggest Mistakes Managers Make*. Prentice Hall, New York, 1997.

[2] Sidney J. Chapman. "Hours of Labour." *Economic Journal*, pages 363–65, September 1909. Footnote 1.

[3] Robert Cialdini. "Perplexing Problem? Borrow Some Brains." *Harvard Management Communication Letter*, August 2004.

[4] Sumantra Ghoshal Heike Bruch. "What Your Weekly Meetings Aren't Telling You." *Harvard Business Review*, volume 80(2), February 2002.

[5] Patrick J. McKenna and David H. Maister. *First among Equals: How to Manage a Group of Professionals*. The Free Press, New York, 2002.

[6] Johanna Rothman. *Corrective Action for the Software Industry*. Paton Press, Chico, CA, 2004.

[7] Peter Senge. *The Fifth Discipline: The Art and Practice of the Learning Organization*. Currency/Doubleday, New York, NY, 1990.

[8] Gerald M. Weinberg. *The Secrets of Consulting*. Dorset House, New York, 1985.

[9] Gerald M. Weinberg. *Quality Software Management: Volume 1, Systems Thinking*. Dorset House Publishing, Inc., New York, 1992.

[10] XP Universe. *Brokering With eXtreme Programming*, 2001. http://www.agileuniverse.com/2001/pdfs/EP201.pdf.

Week Six
Building Capability

Every time you meet one-on-one with the people on your staff, you have an *opportunity* to provide feedback and offer coaching. You have an obligation to provide feedback—it's information your employees need to be successful in their jobs. Coaching is a choice; sometimes yours, and sometimes the employee's.

Coaching provides the help and support for people to improve their capabilities. Employees can request coaching when they want to learn a new skill, when they want to improve their performance, or when they are stuck and need some fresh ideas. As a manager, you may initiate coaching when you see someone struggling or at risk of failure.

You always have the option not to coach. You can choose to give your team member feedback (information about the past), without providing advice on options for future behavior.

Monday Morning

From the first day on the job, Sam noticed that Kevin seemed busy. He seemed not just normal busy—but buried. Kevin was working long hours. Sam knew that long hours usually meant people were tired and making mistakes. But Sam postponed judgment. He wanted to see more of how Kevin worked.

By now, he knew: Kevin was buried. Sam decided it was time to find out what was going on with Kevin.

During their one-on-one, Sam asked, "Kevin, you've been working on this project for a few weeks now, right?"

Kevin nodded and hid a yawn.

"And you're still behind?" Sam asked.

"I'm working overtime to finish it. I still can't keep up. I tried handing off a piece to Joanie, but she didn't do it right. I had to take it back."

"Let's talk about that. How did you decide what work to delegate to Joanie?" *I suspect Kevin doesn't know how to delegate. I wonder whether it was really Joanie, or whether Kevin had a set idea about the method, not just the results,* Sam thought.

Kevin frowned. "I looked at my list. I made a list of everything I didn't want to do, and I looked for people who had time in their schedules. Joanie had the most time, so I asked her to do the work."

"How did that work fit with Joanie's skills?"

"She should know how to do it. She has done work like that in the past. But she didn't do it right. I asked her to check in with me partway though, and I realized she was doing it wrong."

"What was wrong with it?"

"She didn't follow my design, and she didn't implement the interfaces right."

"Would her way have worked?"

Kevin paused. "I guess so. But I wouldn't have done it that way."

"Kevin, you care about finishing the work in a way that meets the customers' needs, right?" Kevin nodded. Sam continued, "Does it matter *how* Joanie works, as long as she delivers the right results in the time you need them?"

Kevin slumped. "Not really."

Sam continued, "Let's talk about how you can delegate your work. I need you to be thinking about the big picture and doing your management work—you can't delegate that part. Let's look at your technical work and see what you can delegate."

"But I like the technical work. I don't want to give it up."

Sam paused, considering what to say. "I'm not sure you have to completely give it up, but look at your task list. Right now, you're on the critical path for the release. What's going to happen if you don't complete these technical tasks in the next two weeks?"

"The release will be late. I don't want that."

"Let's look at who has the skills and the bandwidth to take on these tasks." Sam and Kevin examined Kevin's list of technical tasks.

"Joanie could do these two tasks. And Bill and Andrea can take over these three. They work well together."

Sam and Kevin reviewed the rest of his task list and identified which tasks Kevin could delegate and to whom. That left Kevin with his management tasks and design reviews.

"If I'm not doing technical work, I'm going to lose my technical skills."

Sam had faced this transition himself years ago when he accepted his first management job. He knew that the more people you have in your group, the harder it is to make a technical contribution. Once you have four people or more in your group, you can't perform technical work and still be a great manager.

Sam looked at Kevin. "You've been a technical leader—a product-focused leader. Now you're managing—people-focused leadership. You still need to be involved in product decisions, but you don't need to be the technical lead. It's time to delegate work so you can develop other technical leads in your group.

"How are you going to approach the conversations with Joanie, Bill, and Andrea?" Sam asked.

"I need to talk to Joanie differently than I talk to Bill and Andrea, right?" Kevin said. Sam nodded. Kevin continued, "Well, maybe I'll talk to her first since I didn't get it right the last time."

"You can explain to Joanie that you made a mistake," Sam advised. "Show her that it's okay to admit a mistake. It may sound paradoxical, but admitting you made a mistake makes it easier for people to trust you."

Kevin thought for a moment, steepling his fingers in front of his face. Finally he said, "Here's what I'll say to Joanie:

'Joanie, I want to talk to you about how I assigned you that task and then pulled it back when you were partway through. I was too concerned with *how* you were performing the work, not with your results. I was wrong to pull the work back. I should have let you finish the work. Your way would have worked as well as mine. I'd like to try this again, and I'm going to do it differently this time."'

"That sounds good. You might want to give her a chance to express her thoughts, too. What about Bill and Andrea?"

"Since I haven't blown it with them yet, I can say this: "Bill and Andrea, I need you to do these three tasks. I know you two work well together, so divvy up the work as you will. Take a couple of days to let me know how long you think it will take, and let me know what sort of help you want. We'll track the work in our one-on-ones."

"Excellent. Let me know how it goes next week."

Learning to Delegate

Managers need to focus on managerial work. Some first-level managers still do some technical work, but they cannot assign themselves to the critical path. The point where it's no longer possible to do technical and managerial work depends on the span of management responsibility and the amount of technical work. Giving up technical work is difficult for many technical people because technical work fuels a sense of competence and satisfaction. It's easier to know when technical work is complete than to know when management work is complete.

If you're not sure whether to delegate any of your technical work, review this table to see how much time you *could* devote to technical work.

Decide what you can delegate. Delegating is a primary skill for managers.[3] Consider delegating technical tasks first. Once you've delegated the technical work, look at management tasks: decide which tasks are strategic and which are tactical. For example, selecting the metrics to include on a management report is strategic; gathering the data is tactical. Tactical work is ripe for delegation.[5]

Management Tasks	3 People	4 People
Meeting time: one-on-one meetings, a team meeting, plus some preparation time	4 hours	5 hours
Managing the project portfolio	1 hour	1 hour
Time spent with your manager	1 hour	1 hour
Time spent with peer managers across the organization	1 hour	1 hour
Problem solving with team members (or with project managers or other managers on behalf of team members)	12 hours (4 hours/ person	16 hours (4 hours/ person
Organizational issues	Unpredictable	
Best-case minimum management time	19 hours	24 hours

Figure 6.1: MANAGEMENT TASK TIME

Understand who has the skills to do the work. Look for a match between the skills and aspirations of your staff and the tasks you consider delegating.[8] Consider development opportunities: if someone on your staff wants to move into a leadership role, those tactical tasks may be a great opportunity to begin to understand the management role. (Much of management is strategic work, but starting with the tactical work and moving toward more strategic work can help reduce the learning curve for aspiring managers.) If no one on your staff has the skills or interest to do the work, consider whether you need more people.

Consider delegating an investment. The payoff for delegation isn't always immediate. Don't expect the other person to be 100% productive on a new task. Unless someone has had experience, he or she may not know how to do all aspects of the work. You may still need to coach.[7] Eventually, the investment will result in increased capability and lower risk, because another person understands the task.

Consider the specific results you want. You may have specific deliverables in mind. Or you may be willing to accept a range of results. Communicate the task parameters including time and quality to the person to whom you're delegating. Focus on the results rather than methods.[13] How-to direction is micromanagement.

It takes courage to delegate.[4] It also requires trust. You must trust that other people can do a good enough job, even if they don't do the task quite as well or exactly the way you would.

Decide how the two of you will monitor progress. Establish periodic checks on progress.[3][10] Use frequent checks with less experienced people, and use fewer with those who are more experienced. Provide encouragement, feedback, and help as needed.

Wednesday End of Day

Sam fell in step with Kevin as they walked out of the building into the parking lot. Kevin didn't look quite as tired as he had on Monday. He was standing up straighter, too.

"Hey, Kevin. How's it going? It's nice to see you leaving at a reasonable hour. Your delegation talks went well?"

"Pretty well," Kevin replied. "Joanie grumped a little, but when I admitted I had been wrong, she came around. She has agreed to take on the task. Bill and Andrea are excited about the new challenge. They really like working together. And my wife is happy to have me home for dinner."

"Excellent! I appreciate you having that difficult conversation with Joanie. It took guts to admit a mistake," Sam said.

Notice and Appreciate Changes and Contributions

People crave appreciation. People want to be noticed and appreciated for their contributions.[14] Buckingham and Coffman cite regular recognition as a key factor in retaining the best employees.[2] Notice and appreciate each staff member *every week*.

Notice people doing something right. Look for opportunities to comment on what people are doing well. It doesn't have to be a big

How Many People Can You Manage?

Many newly minted managers live in two worlds: they still have technical work, *and* management responsibilities. Inevitably, the new manager squeezes in management tasks between technical work. And that's creating a high possibility of failure—for the manager and the team.

A minimum list of management tasks for a hypothetical new manager with three or four direct reports is shown in Figure 6.1, on page 97.

Plus, there is time spent on organizational issues (probably in meetings), and ongoing work such as budgets, status reports, email, phone messages, requests for information, and the inevitable task switching. These represent the *minimum* management tasks, and the estimates are optimistic; the minimum management tasks may take more time (unfamiliar tasks always take more time), but they seldom take *less* time.

If there aren't too many organizational problems, the manager with three people on her team may have time for *some* technical work. We strongly recommend managers avoid technical work that's on the critical path—it's a no-win situation. When the manager attends to management work, their technical work suffers; when attending to technical work, the team proceeds without a manager.

With four people in her group, the balance between technical work and management work shifts. In the *best case*, that leaves a whopping sixteen hours to deal with organizational issues *and* complete technical tasks. That's not enough time to do either well.

Maybe you've mastered the technical/management juggling act. You're doing both and even have some slack. It won't last long—people who perform well are asked to do more, and soon have more people and responsibilities.

In our experience, most people don't master the juggling act. Unfortunately, when push comes to shove, technical work trumps management work. For new managers, technical work is more familiar and the consequences of dropping technical tasks are more visible. But dropping management tasks has consequences, too.

deal. Small things such as a well-done report, scripts that work, code that's checked in on time, are worth noticing. We don't buy the notion that "that's just part of the job." Work is difficult, so let people know that you've noticed when they are doing well.

Appreciate, don't thank. Appreciation is different from saying "thank you." "Thank you" may be polite, but it isn't very personal. When you appreciate someone, refer to the person, not just the work.[11] Make appreciations clear and specific—and not an evaluation.

We use this form and modify it as appropriate:

"I appreciate you for _____. It helped me in this way: _____."

Appreciate each of your people every week. Notice and appreciate something about each person who reports to you every week.[6] A one-on-one meeting is a great place to give appreciations.

Choose your venue. Most people don't care about plaques, letters to the personnel file, or public rewards. What they care about is sincere appreciation by their peers[12] and their managers. And, they care whether the sincere appreciation is public or private. When you appreciate someone, decide whether you will appreciate privately or publicly. It's always appropriate to give appreciation for their contribution in a private meeting. If you want to also give public recognition, ask the person, unless you've established this as a norm in your group. When in doubt, ask.[2]

Back to Monday

Ginger strode into Sam's office, ready for her one-on-one. "How's it going, Ginger?" Sam greeted her.

"I've been managing myself," Ginger declared. "I haven't called Marketing idiots all week. I'm making progress!"

"Yep, I've noticed that—that's great. I've also noticed some other things.

"Remember last Tuesday, when you were trying to understand what Marketing really wanted in the release meeting? I saw you roll your eyes, and clench your fists when the Marketing VP was talking. And I heard some loud sighs when the release date came up."

Building Self-awareness

Hierarchy amplifies the impact of words and behavior. One senior manager we know couldn't understand why people were afraid of him. "I'm not a scary person," he shouted, thumping the table with each word.

Managers need to be aware of their own emotional state and how their words and behavior affect other people.

It's perfectly normal to become frustrated or upset with issues at work. It's not okay to yell, scream, swear, rant, rave, or threaten (despite some high-profile examples of this behavior). Even facial expressions can have unintended consequences. A manager who grimaces when she hears a task is late may send the unintended message that she's angry with the messenger. Soon she won't be hearing anything but happy news.

We don't advocate keeping a poker face at all times. People expect managers to have emotions. But if you catch yourself frowning when you hear bad news, let the messenger know you're upset about the news, not at them.

When managers are self-aware, they can *respond* to events rather than *react* in emotional outbursts.

"Oh, yeah. I did all of that. I was really frustrated," Ginger admitted.

"I'm glad you're aware of how your emotions translate into physical reactions. Here's why it's so important for you to manage how you show your frustration. When you sigh, roll your eyes, or clench your fists, you're telegraphing your frustration. People will interpret your frustration in different ways. It's okay to be frustrated. But say that you're frustrated.

"When you *say* you're frustrated," Sam continued, "you can say you're frustrated at the situation, not the person. But unless you tell them, people may think you're mad at them, and they'll be less likely to provide you information—information you need to know."

"Oh, I didn't realize I had that effect on people."

"The higher you are in the organization, the more other people magnify your reactions. That's why it's so important to manage your emotions—not to do away with your emotions, you can't do that—but manage how you express your emotions."

Ginger sighed and then nodded. She realized she had more work to do.

Manage Yourself

Emotions are a part of life: humans are hardwired to have emotions. Acknowledging your emotions explicitly is more productive than telegraphing your emotions through physical displays.[9] Physical displays show you're not ready to hear what the other person has to say. And, physical displays, especially around subordinates, scare people. When you manage how you respond to your own emotional reactions, you make it easier for people to bring you any news, especially bad news.

Awareness is the first step. Become aware of your physical habits and how you display your emotional state. We know many people who drum their fingers, bang the table and grimace and are completely unaware of it. Even your beloved authors don't always know what we're doing that could be driving someone else crazy (our husbands do). Ask someone you trust for feedback. Notice when people have a reaction you don't expect—pulling back from the table, stepping back—and then notice what *you* are doing and what your emotional state is.

Notice triggers. Once you become aware of what you are doing and what's going on inside, notice the situation. Often particular situations trigger emotional and physical reactions. If you've had run-ins with Marketing in the past, you may assume that the next meeting will be a run-in too and prime yourself for an emotional display.

Choose your response. This is easier said than done! Habits are hard to break, especially unconscious physical responses. But awareness of the trigger and your own emotional state provides a starting place. Coaching can be helpful.

Manage your emotions. People who are unable to manage how they express their emotions may need more than coaching. We've heard of people who received Botox injections to keep their emotions off their faces. That's not what we mean. We are people, and people have emotions. Screaming and yelling can be manifestations of emotions. But screaming and yelling are not acceptable outlets for your emotions at work. People who cannot or will not manage themselves should not manage other people.[14]

Obtain feedback about how you appear to others. Select two or three people you trust, and ask for feedback on how you behave and respond in various circumstances. You'll probably hear information that confirms you are managing some tasks and people well. You may also hear some surprising or unsettling information about how other people perceive you. Try to remain open to that feedback—whether you agree, it is the other person's *perception*. Remember that if one person says you have a green tail, he may be seeing things. But if several people say you have a green tail, it's time to look behind you to see what's there.

Keep a journal to help you notice how you respond in different circumstances.

Still Monday

Jason faced a dilemma. Fred, one of his senior developers, was going to leave unless he had an opportunity to try some project management work. Jason knew he needed to discuss career development work with Fred, but he wasn't quite sure how.

"Now that I'm talking to people more often, I'm finding out more about what they want to do. Fred really wants to become a project manager. I don't have a project management job for him, but I don't want him to leave the group. Any ideas?"

"Knowing what people want is the first step. You may not have a project management job right now, but I bet we have a way to help him exercise his project management skills. That way he accomplishes his goals, and we don't lose his domain expertise," replied Sam.

"So, where do I start?"

"What opportunities are there in your group?" asked Sam.

"He could start leading meetings. Tracking his own work as a project would be good, too."

"A lot of what you do in your group is ongoing work. What pieces of work have a clear start and end?" Sam probed.

"Fred could manage the project to write the training for the Ops group."

"Good idea, Jason. That has a clear start and end, and Fred, if he wants to work on his project management skills, can chunk it into small enough pieces that he can monitor progress. I'd suggest you and he create a career development plan. That way you can both make sure he's learning what he wants to learn. What kind of coaching would you like?"

Fred arrived at Jason's office for his one-on-one.

"Fred, you said last week that you wanted to move into project management."

"Yep, I really like seeing a job through from start to finish."

"I think we have a project we can start you with. Remember we talked about moving the training over to Clyde's group? Why don't you organize that as a project and manage it. We'll talk about your progress and what to do when you get stuck."

Fred and Jason developed an action plan for Fred to begin to lead the project. Over the next two months, they tracked his progress during one-on-one meetings. Fred experienced various ups and downs on his first project, but Jason was there as a sounding board and coach. Fred and Jason continued to look for opportunities for Fred to expand his project management experience.

Develop the People in Your Group Every Week

Great managers help each person develop his or her career.[1] Helping people develop skills and achieve their goals increases the overall capacity of the organization. Supporting people to build their careers lets them know you care about them, not just what they produce.

When you assist someone to reach their career goals, he or she will remember you long after leaving your department. We've received great referrals from people we've helped. And many have become valued peers and colleagues.

When you hold people back, they remember that, too—even longer.

Understand what people want. Ask people about their career goals in one-on-ones. Not everyone wants to progress up the hierarchical ladder. Learning a new technical skill or improving written or oral communication increases a person's value to the organization without moving up. Be open to possibilities, and encourage everyone to have learning goals. Seminars, workshops, courses, and book study are all possible ways for people to learn new skills. Support people by allowing some of these activities during work hours.

Create an action plan and follow it. Make a plan with monthly and weekly action steps. Track career development progress in one-on-ones. "Career development" that happens only once a year is a sham.

Look for opportunities to practice new skills. People need to practice new skills before they become proficient. Provide small opportunities for practice with coaching and feedback. Do not expect miracles the first time.

Don't hold people back. Sometimes you can't move people into a new role; the role just does not exist. If that happens, be prepared for the person to move into another department, or even another company. Don't try to hold people back or wait for a new person to backfill the position. Sometimes career development means helping someone find a new position. Holding someone back to make your job easier backfires in the long term.

Create a transition plan. When one of your staff has an opportunity to move elsewhere in the organization, create a transition plan. Transition the person into their new group as quickly as possible. Don't expect the person to continue to perform work in your group.

Separate career development from evaluation. Career development benefits the individual and the organization. But it shouldn't be part of an individual's yearly evaluation or rating. Making space for your staff to develop their careers is part of *your* goal as a manager. You are the one who can ensure that career development is part of daily work.

Career development is different from remedial development. Career development assumes that people are performing their current jobs adequately and are looking for new challenges. When someone can't perform the current job, help him or her learn the job or leave the group.

Now Try This

- Pry your fingers loose from some task you know you need to give up—and delegate it. Review *Setup for Successful Delegation* on page 126.

- Persist with your one-on-ones. Find something to notice and appreciate about each person each week.

- Especially if you haven't started, try coaching one member of your team. Refer to *Guidelines for Effective Coaching* on page 124.

- If you haven't yet, ask two or three trusted people for feedback about how you manage your emotions.

Bibliography for Chapter

[1] David L. Bradford and Allen R. Cohen. *Managing for Excellence: The Guide to Developing High Performance in Contemporary Organizations..* John Wiley & Sons, New York, 1984.

[2] Marcus Buckingham and Curt Coffman. *First, Break All the Rules: What the World's Greatest Managers Do Differently.* Simon and Schuster, New York, NY, 1999.

[3] Clay Carr. *The New Manager's Survival Guide: All the Skills You Need for Success, 2nd Edition.* John Wiley & Sons, New York, 1995.

[4] Stephen R. Covey. *Principle-Centered Leadership.* Summit Books, New York, 1991.

[5] Tom DeMarco. *Slack: Getting Past Burnout, Busywork, and the Myth of Total Efficiency.* Broadway Books, New York, 2001.

[6] Esther Derby. "How to Talk About Work Performance: A Feedback Primer." *Crosstalk*, pages 13–16, December 2003.

[7] Esther Derby. "A Real Go-Getter." *STQE*, volume 5(4), September 2004.

[8] Gerald W. Faust, Richard I. Lyles, and Will Phillips. *Responsible Managers Get Results: How the Best Find Solutions— Not Excuses*. American Management Association, New York, 1998.

[9] Ferdinand F. Fournies. *Coaching for Improved Work Performance*. McGraw Hill, New York, 2000.

[10] Linda A. Hill. *Becoming a Manager: How New Managers Master the Challenge of Leadership*. Penguin Group, New York, 1992.

[11] Naomi Karten. *Communication Gaps and How to Close Them*. Dorset House, New York, 2002.

[12] Steve McConnell. *Rapid Development: Taming Wild Software Schedules*. Microsoft Press, Redmond, WA, 1996.

[13] Johanna Rothman. "Tips for Passing the Baton." *Software Development*, February 2002.

[14] Gerald M. Weinberg. *Quality Software Management, Volume 3: Congruent Action*. Dorset House, New York, 1994.

Week Seven
Dealing with Corporate Realities without Rolling Over

Just when you think everything is all set, something will happen to prove that it's not. You don't have to accept Murphy's Law when it hops onto your projects or into your team; you have other alternatives than to just lie back and accept it.

Tuesday Late Morning

Sam stuck his head in Marty's door.

"Marty, do you have a minute?" Sam asked. "I need to talk to you about a rumor I just heard about the release date."

Marty, Sam's boss, looked up and frowned. "Oh, I was afraid of that. Come on in."

"Is it true we're shortening the schedule by two months?" Sam asked.

"Yes," Marty sighed.

"What's behind the decision to release two months early?"

"You know that big deal we signed with BigCompany? Part of that deal was a release within the next three months. We can't afford a release for them and another for the rest of the customer base, so we decided to do a release for everyone."

Digging Yourself into a Hole

Sometimes we make our own problems. We don't want to ruffle the bosses' feathers, and we shrink from saying "no" directly. When you hear yourself saying these words, you know you are digging yourself a hole that will be hard to climb out of:

- We'll try.

- We should be able to do that.

- Let's hope for the best.

- We'll just do. . . .

- We'll have to make do.

- We'll multitask.

- We'll find resources somewhere.

These sentences all say the same thing: "We can't do this impossible thing, but we'll try it anyway. We'll suck up the risk and postpone a painful discussion until later."

That's a setup for a no-win situation at best and a death-march project at worst. Instead of digging a hole, consider these possibilities:

- I don't know how to do that.

- I won't promise something I know I cannot deliver. Here's what I believe we can deliver.

- I will work with my team to see what we can achieve.

- We'll work on the most important features first and show you each month what we've completed.

The conversation that ensues probably won't be pleasant. But both you and your manager will be dealing with reality. Waiting to have the conversation only delays the pain and reduces the number of options available to meet business goals.

He looked hard at Sam. "A ton of revenue is riding on it. And if they like this release, we could end up with an even bigger deal."

Sam knew he needed to understand how the new deal with Big-Company would change the priorities of the release.

Sam nodded and said, "It's not just that we have to get the release out; we have to get it out in good shape, at least for what BigCompany wants to do." Marty nodded. "What about the rest of the customers? Do we need to make it available to everyone else?"

"A bunch of the features we're doing are just for BigCompany. But the cleanup we're doing on half-baked features from the last release—so our operations costs decrease—that's important for us and the other customers."

"Can you give me the list of what we promised BigCompany?"

"I'll forward you the agreement."

Sam asked more questions about specific features to understand the priorities and expectations set with BigCompany.

"I'm going to work with my team to understand how, in the time we have, we can meet those expectations. I'll let you know in a few days what we think we can accomplish, and then you and I can jointly decide how to prioritize what we work on first and what may fall off the plate."

"Nothing can fall off the plate!" Marty growled.

"I'd like to be able to give you everything you want. But we originally estimated we needed five months, and now we have three months. Until I talk to my team, I can't guarantee what we'll be able to deliver."

"You have a product to deliver. I don't want excuses or guarantees. I want product," Marty said.

Me, too, Sam thought. *I can't blame Marty for wanting what he wants. I'm not going to argue with him—that would be pointless. I need to first work with my team to see what we can deliver.*

◇◇◇

Manage Your Boss, Stand Up for Your Team

Senior management and other groups in an organization may want you to perform heroic acts, but taking on more work than you can handle isn't heroism; it's martyrdom. When you take on work you can't handle, you take on all the risk (and generally, none of the reward).

Understand the other person's context. Don't blame the other person (in this case, a senior manager) for wanting what they want. Understand the reasons and needs behind the desire.[5][1]

Avoid premature decisions. When senior management informs you the plan has taken a 180-degree turn, they often want to know right away that you can meet the new agenda. It's tempting to rise to the challenge. The "simple" answers—add more staff, work overtime, multitask, "think outside the box"—don't work. If you hear yourself saying, "We'll just do blah, blah, blah," Stop! "Just" is a keyword that lets you know it just won't work.

Don't agree to a deliverable before you talk to your team.[1] Work with your team to discover what is possible.[7] Promising to "find a way" without consulting with your team sets everyone up for failure. Saying "no" without looking into the request puts you at odds with your boss and reduces your ability to negotiate.[3]

Respect the *request* without making a promise. Be firm, stating that you can't commit until you discuss what is possible with your team.

Review options, and report back. Expect to report back in a day or two. It's unlikely that a senior manager who is experiencing pressure will agree to more time than that. Promise to communicate what your team believes they can deliver at the end of that period.

Work with your team to develop some credible options.[3] Simply mandating extended overtime[4] and indiscriminately adding more people[2] to the team are not credible options. When you have no credible option and management won't budge, remember that finding another job is always an alternative.

Tuesday Just Before Noon

Sam sent an email to his management team.

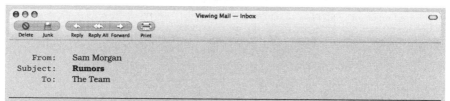

From: Sam Morgan
Subject: **Rumors**
To: The Team

The rumor we heard about the release date is true. The next release ships in three months. It's not a whim; Marty has good reasons to make this change. The BigCompany sale hinges on delivering early.

We need to respond to this change. We're going to have to deliver something. We need to determine what that "something" can be.

Based on my initial look at the list, I see a fair amount of overlap, but we'll still have to make some changes. We need input from the technical staff in order to replan. Please work with the technical folks to develop preliminary sizings. We need the estimates to do the replanning.

I'm sure people have already heard the rumor. Reassure them that this doesn't mean a death march or tons of overtime. Request their help–we need it–to develop reasonable estimates. Once they're done working on estimates, have folks wrap up current work as best they can. We'll be redirecting people when we know what the plan is.

I'm sure some of the dependencies are going to change, so start people thinking about that, too.

I'm scheduling a 1/2 day in the morning to work out the details. We'll meet in Conference Room A so we can see our current 4-week plan.

I promised Marty we'd have a plan to him by day after tomorrow.

See you in Conference Room A at 9 AM. I'll stop by to talk with each of you early this afternoon to answer questions.

I've attached the feature list Marty gave me.

Sam

After Lunch

Sam made a quick circuit of the office to make sure each of the managers received the news and to answer questions.

"Aren't we just going to work overtime?" asked Kevin, resigned to the inevitable.

"Nope," said Sam. "Overtime makes people tired, and tired people make more mistakes. We can't afford mistakes, so we're not going to do something we know will hurt us more than help us. Even if we worked overtime, we couldn't accomplish everything.

"We'll replan to make sure we're working on the highest-priority items, according to Marty's list. We'll manage expectations with Marty so he's not surprised by what's in and what's out.

Thursday

Thursday morning, Sam strode to Marty's office, plan in hand.

"Marty, I've spent the last two days working with my team to replan this release. We focused on the most important features based on the list you gave us. We've organized it and reorganized it and arrived at an achievable plan. These are the features we're going to work on." Sam handed Marty the list. Sam waited a minute while Marty scanned the list. "Not all the features originally planned for this release are on the list, but the most important ones for BigCompany are."

Marty examined the list. "Is this the best you can do?"

"Yes. We've spent the last two days figuring out how to get this much done. If you see a better way, let me know."

"Couldn't you just add these two features back in?" Marty asked.

"Not and meet the release date. We know what our capacity is, and we're at it."

"I better talk to the sales guy if this is the best you can do. What if you put everyone on overtime? Or hire more people?" Marty asked.

"The learning curve is too steep. If we hire people now, they won't be up to speed before the release date. And extended overtime—three months—would guarantee the developers make too many mistakes and the testers will be too tired to find them.

"I'd be happy to talk to the sales guys with you," Sam finished.

Marty harrumphed but agreed.

◇◇◇

Leading Your Team through a Change in Priorities

Change is inevitable. Markets shift, customers leave, and new deals cause changes in direction. The more visibility you have into current work, the easier it is to adapt to changes.

Replace rumors with facts. When you hear a rumor that could affect the work of your group, track it down. Don't leave people to stew or replace the lack of information with their worst fears. As soon as you know the facts, tell your team, and lead the effort to adapt to the change.

Set your team's expectations about how you will respond to the change. Teams who are accustomed to "simple answers," such as add bodies, work overtime, and multitask, are likely to fall into that pattern—unless you model another option. Show the team how to work through the implications of the change. Show how to generate and analyze sensible options, and then replan based on the best option available. Changing habits takes time and education.

Replan with your team. Don't commit without involving your team. Making big promises without consulting the people who do the work destroys trust.

Now Try This

- Review your manager's patterns. Some managers have lots of great ideas, and forget about them as soon as the words are spoken. We taught one such manager to hold up a red card when he was "just thinking out loud" and a green one when he was seriously discussing a new initiative. That doesn't work with every manager. Sometimes, your best bet is to verbally agree and not do the work. Formulate a hypothesis on how your boss treats his flow of ideas. Then observe, gather data (including asking direct questions), and agree upon a strategy of how you'll handle new candidate initiatives.

- Review the patterns in your organization. Create a chart that shows how often delivery dates change. What are the reasons behind the changes? How often are the new dates actually met? What happens to the people involved when dates are not met? What happens to the bottom line? What does this tell you about possible strategies the next time your boss tells you the delivery date is changing?

- The next time you find yourself in this situation, see the sidebar on page 71 and *Solving Problems: Create New Situations* on page 154 to develop alternative approaches for accomplishing the work.

Epilogue

Sam leaned back, and stretched. *Well, we did it. We finished the release. Didn't complete everything Marty wanted, but we did enough to make sure the customer would be happy. And we didn't burn anyone out doing it—because the team applied good management principles.*

Just then, Marty popped his head in. "Your team really pulled through for us," Marty said. "You lit a fire under this group."

Lighting a fire is not how management works, Sam thought. "They are a bright group. They care about their jobs and the company. All I did was create an environment for them to succeed."

"I don't know what magic you did, but it's working," Marty said. "They would follow you anywhere. You'd better stay here for a while."

Sam smiled.

What Management Is

Management exists to organize purposefully.[6] The whole purpose is to deliver results and build capacity. It's conceptually easy but operationally difficult.

Apply simple—but not easy—practices consistently. None of the practices described here—one-on-ones, portfolio management, feedback, coaching, delegation—is difficult to understand. They are simple practices. But the key to successful management is to consistently and reliably perform those practices.

Managers who never apply these practices are poor managers.

Managers who apply these practices intermittently are only average managers.

Great managers consistently and reliably apply all these management practices.

Learn about your staff as people. No matter where you are in the organization's hierarchy, it's important to understand the people with whom you work. It may seem paradoxical, but the higher a manager is in the hierarchy, the more important it is to know people *as people*.

Work with other managers as a team. Working as a management team allows all the managers to see where the department's problems and successes are. A management team will reduce the likelihood that one manager will solve problems in ways that create problems for another manager.

If your peer group of managers isn't working as a team, start having conversations with your peers to find ways to work together to accomplish department goals. Learn about areas where goals conflict so you can influence *your* manager to organize your peer group into a management team.

Develop shared goals. The most successful departments we've seen have management teams that share goals at each level. The first-level managers share goals. The mid-level managers share goals. And the senior managers share goals. The more each manager understands about his or her peer managers' goals, the more likely each manager will be to work so that others can achieve their goals.

Explain the goals. We meet many managers who tell us their goals are to reduce time to market, reduce cost, or increase market share. Goals like these are a good starting point, but they are too vague. Make goals useful by making them SMART (see *Setting SMART Goals* on page 138). Take every opportunity to explain the goals to your team. When people know what the goals are, they tend to accomplish them.

Define what success means. If *your* manager hasn't defined a mission and a strategy for your group, create one—with the help of the people in your group. Use the mission and strategy to develop a definition of success. Once you know what success is, identify (and complete) actions to achieve success.

Tackle the highest-priority work. The best way to deliver results and increase capacity is by working on—and completing—high-priority work. The low-priority work (and the work on your not-to-do list) reduces the energy available for the high-priority work. Completing the highest-priority work helps your team feel as if they've accomplished something useful.

Help people work together effectively. Sometimes people who have never been in a management role believe that managers can simply tell other people what to do and that's that. Not so. Much of management work is facilitative, not directive. Facilitate people working together by discovering common interests, discussing possible solutions (before surprising people with them in a meeting), using the sidebar on page 71 to generate multiple options, and clarifying decision rules. Effective managers don't just tell other people what to do; they help other people work together.

Create an environment of trust. Consistent management (provided it's not consistently bad management) creates trust. In an environment of trust, people work diligently and work for the good of the organization.

Now Try This

- Review the practices you've adopted. See whether you can you detect any changes in your work and your group's work.

- Review the practices you have not yet adopted. Consider how those practices might change the work you and your group achieve. What's preventing you from adopting these practices?

- Review your management journal. Look for trends or evidence that you are accomplishing more of the important work and reducing the amount of effort expended on low-priority work in your group. Check to see whether you're surprised by work. If you're still surprised by work or still performing work that should be on your not-to-do list, influence your peers to arrive at common goals.

- As you review your management journal, look for times you are effectively managing yourself and times when you are not. What's different in each situation?

Bibliography for Chapter

[1] Mary Albright and Clay Carr. *101 Biggest Mistakes Managers Make*. Prentice Hall, New York, 1997.

[2] Frederick P. Brooks, Jr. *The Mythical Man Month: Essays on Software Engineering*. Addison-Wesley, Reading, MA, anniversary edition, 1995.

[3] Esther Derby. "If at First, and Last, You Don't Succeed." *STQE*, volume 4(5), September 2002.

[4] Gene Fellner, editor. *Unreported and Upaid Overtime: Distorted Measurements and Formulas for Failure*. Pearson Education, Boston, 2002.

[5] John J. Gabarro and John P. Kotter. "Managing Your Boss." *Harvard Business Review*, pages 92–100, January 1980.

[6] Joan Magretta and Nan Stone. *What Management Is: How It Works and Why It's Everyone's Business*. Free Press, New York, NY, 2002.

[7] Johanna Rothman. "Successful Software Management: Fourteen Lessons Learned." *Crosstalk*, pages 17–20, December 2003.

Techniques for Practicing Great Management

So, you're ready to start trying some of the ideas you've seen in this book. We'd like to share some tips, techniques, and checklists we've collected and used over the years to get you started.

But remember that management is not a simple step-by-step activity. Going through the motions without a genuine interest in people and an understanding of priorities won't work. That said, checklists, techniques, and clear-cut guidance can be the first step toward mastery.

Working with Your Team

Throughout the book, Sam interacts with the people who report to him in team meetings and one-on-one meetings. He coaches, provides feedback, and delegates tasks.

For guidance on when and how to coach and keys for effective feedback and effective delegation, see these sections:

- *Guidelines for Effective Coaching*, on page 124
- *Guide to Giving Effective Feedback*, on page 134
- *Setup for Successful Delegation*, on page 126

Much of the time, Sam works with people in meetings. For information on improving one-on-one and team meetings, see these sections:

- *Making One-on-Ones Work*, on page 150

- *Run Effective Meetings*, on page 143

- *Facilitation Essentials for Managers*, on page 128

Part of managing lies in building relationships and understanding what's happening in the group; take advantage of informal opportunities to build relationships and gather information. Walking around and listening to people is a great way to learn what's going on with your group.

Now it may seem like there's no way to do this wrong. But alas, many managers have annoyed the people who report to them by plopping down in a team member's office and offering advice or by standing behind someone's chair waiting for a phone conversation to end. A little etiquette is in order. The finer points of MBWAL are found in

- *Manage by Walking Around & Listening*, on page 142

Part of managing others is being ready for new hires. If you'd like to streamline your activities when you hire someone new, see

- *Welcoming New Hires*, on page 136

Working within the Organizational Context

Sam helped his group become more effective by clearly articulating goals and focusing efforts on the most important work within the context of their group and their company.

If you want to do this for your group, read

- *Setting SMART Goals*, on page 138

- *Project Portfolio Planning Tips*, on page 156

Using formal authority may work sometimes—though not as often as you might think. Most of the time, influence and lateral relationships contribute to accomplishing goals. (Even within your group, influence is more effective than "pulling rank.")

Brush up on the basics of influence in

- *Preparing for Influence*, on page 153

Working on Yourself

Managers are people, too, and sometimes our communications go awry, or we become stuck. For a quick look at the internal process of communication, read:

- *What Goes on Inside our Heads*, on page 140

And when you need some suggestions to start the creative juices on a tough problem, try

- *Solving Problems: Create New Situations*, on page 154

Technique:
Guidelines for Effective Coaching

Part of a manager's job is to coach his or her direct reports to increase their capability and effectiveness within the organization. Coaching can focus on either interpersonal skills or technical work that is relevant to the job.

Coaching is different from feedback and from mentoring. As a manager, you are obligated to provide feedback when someone is not performing some aspect of his or her job. Mentoring is a voluntary relationship that works better when there isn't a reporting relationship. Coaching is part of your choice as a manager to help people increase some capability.

Coaching is part of a manager's job, too, but coaching focuses on increasing skills and capability. You may coach someone who has decided to work on a performance issue, or you may coach to develop new skills and insights. In either case, coaching is a helping relationship, so make sure the other person wants your help. Advice inflicted without consent is seldom valued. Unless you can answer "yes" to all the questions in Figure 8.1, refrain from inflicting help.

Questions to ask yourself:	Yes	No
Could this person be more effective if he or she made some changes?	☐	☐
Is the coaching about the technical work or the behaviors related to the job?	☐	☐
Does this person want to work on this area?	☐	☐
Is this person willing to accept your help?	☐	☐

Figure 8.1: COACHING CHECKLIST

Guidelines for coaching:

- Make sure you've provided timely and effective feedback.

- Ask whether the person wants coaching or offer to provide helpful information.

- Engage in conversation to articulate how new skills or behaviors would increase effectiveness.

- Discuss additional options, alternatives, or strategies. People usually choose the best alternative they know—but may have a limited repertoire. Coaching helps increase the range of effective options from which to choose. We have found questions like these help people generate options:

  - What problem are you trying to solve?

  - What are the benefits of taking that option?

  - What could go wrong if you take that option?

  - Who else is affected by that option?

  - What alternatives did you consider?

  - What are two other ways to accomplish this goal?

  - How could we make the situation worse?

  - If we could do only one small thing, what would it be?

  - How would an engineer, marketing person, salesperson, or tester (choose a role different from your role) look at this?

  - Where do we get the greatest leverage?

- Discuss the implications of each option. Don't lead to a particular outcome; instead, encourage exploration of each option from the perspective of the person you are coaching. Share your perspective but allow the person you are coaching to select the option that suits his or her needs.

- Develop an action plan.

- Follow up each week in your one-on-one meeting. Recognize successes. Analyze less successful attempts at trying new skills and behaviors. Look for ways to refine and enhance what did work and correct what didn't.

Technique:
Setup for Successful Delegation

You can't do everything by yourself. The time will come when you'll need to delegate managerial or technical tasks to other people. (Don't think of it as shirking your duties; you're providing opportunities to others).

To determine whether a situation is amenable to delegation, begin by asking yourself the questions shown in Figure 8.2, on the facing page.

Guidelines

- Choose your delegatee wisely. Select someone who wants to take on more responsibility and who has identified areas of career development where this work would fit. Don't select someone who is not interested in the work you want to delegate.

- Articulate your expectations about the work: what's acceptable when you need it.

- Clarify any unacceptable solutions.

- Define interim milestones. If you've delegated a decision, recognize that a decision has at least two parts: generating alternatives and choosing an alternative. Clarify what part(s) you are delegating, and be explicit if you really want a checkpoint between the two parts.

Questions to ask yourself:	Yes	No
Is it a discrete chunk of work?	☐	☐
Does the person have the skills to do the work?	☐	☐
Does the person have the authority to be successful?	☐	☐
Does the person have the tools necessary to be successful?	☐	☐
Does the person know what the results should look like?	☐	☐
Does the person know when the work is due?	☐	☐
Do you know how often you want this person to report on progress?	☐	☐
Does this person know what progress looks like?	☐	☐
Is this work too risky to delegate?	☐	☐
Have you set the boundary conditions, e.g. budget, time, and other resources or constraints, for the work?	☐	☐
Do you have a format for the work product you want this person to use?	☐	☐

Figure 8.2: DELEGATION CHECKLIST

Technique:

Facilitation Essentials for Managers

Facilitation means providing a process and structure to help a group think and solve problems together. As a manager, you may have to help the group develop ideas, consider options, and choose a solution.

Make Sure the Meeting Has a Goal

When you design and facilitate a meeting, it's important to have a goal. The goal needs to be specific enough to focus the participants on the current issue, but not so specific that it constrains the outcome. These are some examples of "broad enough" goals are:

- Identify practical ways to improve our build process.
- Generate possible ways to overcome the impasse in vendor negotiations.

Facilitation is not directing a group toward a specific outcome. If you have a preconceived outcome in mind and want to guide a group to reach that conclusion, facilitation is not the proper tool. "Facilitating" a discussion toward a preconceived outcome feels manipulative to the people in the process.

Facilitation will help the group identify the steps necessary to reach the goal, and how the group will accomplish each step (the process).

As a manager facilitating a working group or team, you'll need these skills to help the group:

- Generate and integrate ideas
- Evaluate options
- Test agreement
- Participate

Generate and Integrate Ideas

Traditional brainstorming. This aims to spark creativity and generate many ideas in a short time. The guidelines for brainstorming are as follows:

- Everyone participates.
- Write down *all* ideas for the entire group to see.
- No discussing the ideas—compliments or criticism—during the brainstorming.
- It's okay to build on others' ideas.
- No idea is too wild or too silly.

Start by stating the focus of the brainstorm. Review the guidelines, and set a time limit. At the end of the brainstorm, allow time for clarifying questions. Prioritize the list to identify the most useful ideas.

Silent brainstorming. Traditional brainstorming favors people who enjoy thinking "on their feet" and who are comfortable shouting out their ideas in a group. People who need a bit of time to gather their thoughts or who aren't comfortable talking over people to get their ideas heard don't do as well with traditional brainstorming. And that means the group is missing some good ideas.

Silent brainstorming allows for silent individual thinking before the whole group sees the ideas.

Procedure:

1. State the topic focus, review the process, and set a time limit.

2. Allow five to ten minutes for each person to jot down at least ten ideas related to the topic. Ask for at least ten ideas.

3. Form pairs to discuss the ideas. Have each pair identify their best ideas and transfer them to large index cards. Do the math so that you end up with about thirty-five ideas; e.g. for a group of fourteen, have each pair select five ideas.

4. Post the cards on a wall for all to see. There will be duplicates, and that's okay.

(For more information on this process, see Stanfield.[10])

Affinity grouping. Organizing the cards allows categories and key ideas to emerge from a raw unorganized list of ideas, such as the list from traditional or silent brainstorming. Affinity grouping helps the group see relationships between ideas and integrate them. It also moves the group from "my idea" toward "our idea."

Use this after traditional or silent brainstorming.

1. Ask the group which ideas seem related, and move those cards close together. Continue asking the question and moving the cards until all the cards are in clusters.

2. Name the clusters. The names of the clusters represent the consensus of the group around a particular idea.

When the facilitator moves the cards around, conversations about the groupings happens publicly, and most of the group will stay engaged. When the group is left on their own to arrange the cards into affinity groups, inevitably one or two people dominate. The result is that the thought process is not open to all, and the rest of the group disengages.

Evaluating Options

There is no one right way to evaluate options. Dozens (hundreds!) of techniques are available. We find the simple ones usually work best. Before you start the evaluation, write down and post the key ideas of each option. Review each alternative, and allow time for clarifying questions. Don't assume people know the definitions of the options—one of the most common reasons for disagreement is that people have different understandings of alternative or different definitions for words. Keep the summaries posted during the evaluation in case you need to refer to them.

Evaluate each option *on its own* before comparing options to each other.

Draw two lines on a piece of flip-chart paper (this creates three columns). List the pros and cons of the options in the first two columns. Note what's interesting about the option in the third column.[1] Answer all three questions for one alternative before moving to the next.

After the group has completed this activity for all the options, it's obvious which ideas are suitable and which are not.

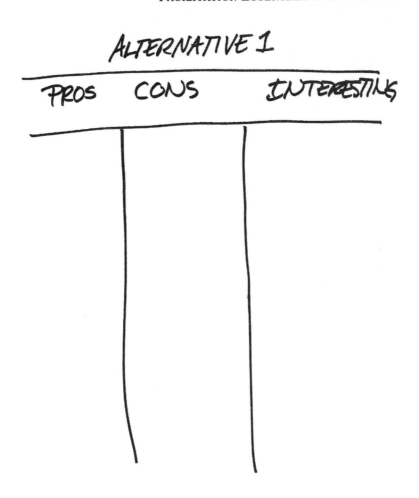

Figure 8.3: ALTERNATIVE EVALUATION

Testing Agreement

Teams need a way to test their agreement, discuss concerns, and reach a decision that all can support.

Roman Evaluation plays on the sign that the ancient Romans used to signal their pleasure with fighters in the gladiator ring. In modern use, this technique actually *prevents* bloody, gladitorial-style fights. This method provides more information on the level of support than a simple up/down vote.

These are the signals:

- Thumbs up = "I support this proposal."
- Thumbs sideways = "I'll abide by the will of the group."
- Thumbs down = "I do not support this proposal and wish to speak."

Ask each person to vote with his or her thumb. If all thumbs are down, you can eliminate the option.

When votes are mixed, allow time for the people with reservations to state their views. They may have important information that will change the opinions of others in the group. A word of caution: the point is not for people to advocate, persuade, or browbeat—it's simply to bring more information into consideration.

When a large part of the group is "thumb sideways"—they'll abide by the will of the group—support for the option is at best, luke-warm, which is reason for caution.

Roman Evaluation works toward consensus. Consensus means that everyone must be willing to support the idea, even if it's not his personal first choice. Consensus is not a majority vote.

How to handle the lone holdout. Consensus has its downsides. Sometimes one person can hold up any movement by vetoing every proposal. The best time to handle this situation is before it starts. Set a time limit and a fallback decision rule. Some options for fallback rules are:

- Turn the decision over to some outside person or group.
- Take a vote.
- Make the decision yourself on the basis of the group input.

People don't hold out to be obstinate. Most have a deeply held principle behind their position. Respect the belief, and use your fallback decision rule to continue.

A caution about voting. Majority vote is quick. And sometimes, when the stakes are low, it's the best way to reach a decision. When you need the group to fully support a decision, building consensus saves time in the long run.

Help Everyone Participate

You don't have to be in the front of the room to use any of these strategies. Techniques that help group dynamics are as follows:

Ask for a progress check. For example, if the session ends in twenty minutes and there are still five agenda items, say "I notice that we only have twenty minutes left. Can we concentrate on prioritize the remaining items since we can probably finish only two?"

Make room for others to speak. If you see another person trying unsuccessfully to break into the conversation, say "It looks like Jody has something to say" or "Were you about to say something, Jody?" You can also help when there's a chronic interrupter in the room by saying something such as "I think we may have interrupted Joe before he was finished. Joe?"

Restate using different words. Sometimes stating an idea in different words can help when someone is stuck on particular point: "I hear you saying XYZ. Do I have it about right?" Rephrasing helps people feel heard and understood.

Comment on what you see. If the group keeps returning to topics or decisions that seemed closed, comment on it: "I notice that we're talking about Topic X again. Do we need to reopen that, or can we move back to Topic Y?"

Summarize. Summarizing important points can help the group move forward: "Here's what I've heard us agree to. Is that correct?" If people don't agree with your summary, you've just saved much future aggravation by surfacing the misunderstanding.

At the end of every session, review action items. Make sure people understand and agree with their action items, what the deliverables are, and when they are due.

As the facilitator, you are responsible for the process, not the outcome. Facilitate only when you don't need to contribute content to the discussion. It's not possible to facilitate effectively and participate effectively at the same time.

Consider an outside facilitator when the stakes are high or you have content to contribute.

Technique:

Guide to Giving Effective Feedback

People (including you) need to know what they're doing well and what they need to change to be successful. Use these steps for positive feedback, too. Provide people with specific information about what they should continue, as well as what they could do differently.

We use the six-step process for feedback shown in Figure 8.4, on the next page.[3]

Guidelines:

- Be specific. No one can act on hints or vague feedback. Telling a person "This report is exceptional" may impart a glow but doesn't help the person understand what was exceptional. "The table of contents made it very easy for me to find what I was looking for in this report" is more likely to result in more exceptional reports in the future.

- Provide feedback as close to the event as possible. Waiting until a year-end review is not helpful. Even waiting until a quarter-end is not helpful.

- Don't label the person; describe the behavior or result. So instead of saying "Your work is sloppy," say "I noticed the last set of release notes, contained typing and spelling errors."

- Don't blame the person; describe specifics. Instead of "You never test your code," say "When you checked these last three changes in, you didn't test the changes."

- Check to make sure the feedback recipient agrees that your description (observable behavior or results) is correct. When the feedback recipient doesn't agree with your data, he or she will check out of the conversation and certainly won't change behavior.

1. Check whether this is a necessary item for feedback: Does it affect the work? Does it affect working relationships? If not, don't bother with feedback.

2. Prepare to give the feedback. Gather specific examples of recent instances of the problem. Focus on behavior or results.

3. Determine the outcome you desire. Be ready to give corrective feedback or coaching.

4. Deliver feedback privately. Deliver "normal" feedback (appreciations, corrective or coaching feedback) in one-on-ones. When someone is close to losing his or her job, call a separate meeting so the person understands the gravity of the situation.

5. If you have some specific action or result you want, say it. If you're open to a range of possible solutions, engage in joint problem solving.

6. Agree how you'll follow up.

Figure 8.4: SIX-STEP PROCESS FOR FEEDBACK

Technique:
Welcoming New Hires

Bringing people into your group is not trivial. Use or adapt the checklists shown here to help new hires settle into their new positions quickly and efficiently. (Excerpt courtesy Johanna Rothman/Dorset House.[7])

☐ Order a badge, keys, and keycards, as needed.

☐ Identify suitable office space, and verify that the space is clean and ready for a new occupant.

☐ Verify that the chosen office is equipped with a desk, lamp, chair, phone, and all necessary computer equipment, and that all are in working order.

☐ Order any needed furniture, office supplies, or computer equipment missing from the chosen office.

☐ Requisition an e-mail address, a voicemail connection, and a physical mailbox.

Figure 8.5: ACTIVITIES TO COMPLETE UPON OFFER ACCEPTANCE

- ☐ Stock the office with basic office supplies, such as pens, paper, pencils, wastebasket, scissors, stapler, staples, and staple remover.

- ☐ Verify e-mail access and computer hook-up to the network.

- ☐ Verify that phone and e-mail directories and a location map are available and add the employee's voicemail extension to the phone list.

- ☐ Document the locations of the applications and templates for the employee's work.

- ☐ Supply the employee with hardcopy manuals, as applicable to his or her work, or provide information on electronic access.

- ☐ Assign a buddy who can be available for the first month or so to answer the new hire's technical questions about how the team works and non-technical questions about staff, neighborhood, rules, and traditions peculiar to the specific environment and culture.

- ☐ Prepare a welcome letter and orientation package, including all HR forms.

Figure 8.6: ACTIVITIES IN PREPARATION FOR THE FIRST DAY

- ☐ Add the employee's name and title to the organization chart; add the name and extension number to the phone directory, and other relevant lists.

- ☐ Introduce the new hire to project, executives, personnel, administrative staff, as needed.

Figure 8.7: ACTIVITIES FOR NEW HIRE'S ARRIVAL ON DAY ONE.

Technique:
Setting SMART Goals

People need to know where they're headed to make the daily and weekly decisions about their work without having to come to you. When they don't have goals, each person chooses his or her own priorities. They may not be your priorities, and they may not mesh with co-workers' priorities or organizational priorities. People make choices based on what they like to do, what's easiest, what's most challenging, what helps their friends the most, and all kinds of reasons—reasons that don't necessarily match the company's needs.

Guidelines

For setting group goals, consider using a technique called *affinity grouping*.

1. Frame the question. Here are possibilities:

   • What problems did we encounter in the last project?

   • What problems have we encountered over the last few months?

   • Where do we want to be in six months?

   • How do we accomplish this goal of increasing revenue in the next six months?

2. Write down one answer or idea per sticky.

3. Post the stickies on a wall, and group them by common theme.

4. Label each grouping.

5. As a group, develop actions that will help you achieve the goals stated in each theme.

Set individual goals in a one-on-one. Individual goals are complementary to the group goals and are tied to the group's mission. In addition, individual goals address each person's specific issues and may include career development goals.

Individual and team goals support the mission of the group—the reason the department exists.

Make goals SMART: Specific, Measurable, Attainable, Relevant, and Time-bound. Here's an example of a goal that isn't SMART: "Improve product quality." Here's a SMART version of that goal: "Decrease the total number of released defects in the next release by 10%."

Technique:
What Goes on Inside our Heads

Great managers acknowledge that they—and other people—have emotional reactions to situations at work. We hear people make statements such as "He makes me angry." It's more accurate to say: "My interpretation of his behavior makes me angry." Understanding the source of your reactions allows you to manage your response.

Here is a model of interaction we find useful.[5]

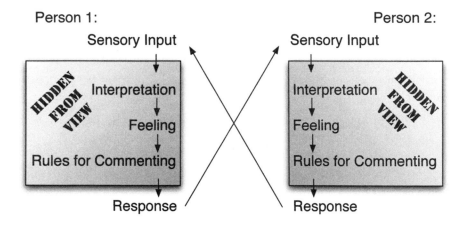

Figure 8.8: SATIR INTERACTION MODEL.

Sensory input. We take in information through our senses. We hear words, tone, and inflection. We see facial expressions, gestures, and posture.

Interpretation. We attach meaning to the words and other information based on associations and past experience.

Feeling. We have a feeling based on the interpretation we've made.

Rules for commenting. We may have rules about what we can say and what we keep to ourselves (e.g., "If you can't say anything nice, don't say anything at all.")

Response. We respond based on our interpretation, feelings, and rules about commenting—and the other person is unaware of all these! Is it any wonder that some interactions are puzzling?

Guidelines

When you feel a strong emotion, check the facts of the situation and search for hidden assumptions. Make a point to test your assumptions—are they really true? Articulate how you interpret the facts. Are there other interpretations?

If you have a strong physical response, you're probably having a strong emotional response.

Keep a journal of events or situations that seem to provoke a strong response for you. You may be able to detect patterns.

Technique:
Manage by Walking Around & Listening

MBWAL helps give you a richer view of your team's work. You'll be able to see and hear how people are working, including their moods and morale. MBWAL also gives you a chance to talk to people informally.

Guidelines

- Tell people you're going to leave your office and circulate. Let them know that you'll be asking them questions.

- Leave your office and walk around. Aim for once or twice a week. Daily is great, but we've never met a manager who had the time every day to wander. How long you spend mingling depends. Five minutes is probably not enough. An hour is probably too much.

- Listen to the current conversations.

- Don't interrupt people who are on the phone or who seem to be working intently. One thing we've done is use do-not-disturb signs or red/green flags for people who don't want to be disturbed. This works for other people as well as for you.

- Take your notebook to record action items. As you circulate, people will ask you questions. Record your action items, and let people know when you'll have an update. Be careful about walking around silently taking notes. That looks like spying.

- Notice what people ask you. Their questions are a clue about their concerns. It shows you areas where people don't know how to obtain information for themselves or where your communication may be weak.

Technique:
Run Effective Meetings

General Meeting Tips

Meetings can be an effective way to accomplish group work. But meetings have a bad reputation, largely because there are so many bad meetings. It doesn't have to be that way. Most companies could realize significant productivity gains—without fancy methodologies and high-priced consultants—if they put only a little effort into improving their meetings.

Figure 8.9, on the following page shows our template for organizing a meeting.

The *Role* in the figure describe how people may participate. You may require a facilitator, a moderator, a scribe, or a timekeeper. If you will be requesting that people serve specific roles, this is where you define them.

Guidelines

Meetings create value when people do the following:

- Plan work.
- Solve problems.
- Reach decisions.
- Share pertinent information.
- Provide answers to questions.

If there's no specific purpose for a particular meeting, the meeting serves no purpose. Cancel it.

Use meetings for multidirectional exchange of information. Serial status reporting—where several people working on largely independent initiatives report status to a manager—aren't multidirectional exchanges. Serial status reporting may *appear* to save time for the manager, but wastes everyone else's time. And because everyone is so disgusted with the meeting, they complain about it before and after. That's a waste of time for everyone.

MEETING
AGENDA
TEMPLATE

MEETING PURPOSE:
(the reason you've asked people to
spend their valuable time with
you)

EXPECTED ATTENDEES:
(the people who will make the
decision(s) to solve the problem(s))

GOAL:
(what you expect to accomplish
by the end of the meeting)

AGENDA:
(the steps you will use to reach
the goal)

ROLES:
(any special roles, e.g., facilitator,
scribe)

Figure 8.9: MEETING ORGANIZATION TEMPLATE

Make sure the right people are in the room (and only the right people are in the room). One of the reasons so many meetings are a waste of time is that either:

a) the group attempts to plan or make a decision without the people needed to provide information or represent interests or

b) there are too many people who represent peripheral interests.

Issues and problems that are vital to the organization's interests provoke interest. Many people who are interested but not accountable for the outcome will want to attend. When the organization trusts that other people can arrive at reasonable decisions, they won't feel compelled to attend; they'll know they'll receive pertinent information in a timely fashion.

But before people learn that trust, it's not always possible (or even politic) to exclude interested people from the room. The most effective way to handle people who are interested but not accountable is to give them a formal role.

Create a formal Observer role. Observers attend meetings to listen and learn, not participate. Emphasize the difference in their role by having them sit away from the meeting table.

If an Observer insists on participating, take one of these actions:

- Explain how the meeting outcome will be communicated and ask them (politely) to leave.

- Clarify meeting roles, rules, and outcomes at the beginning of the meeting. Clarify who owns the final decision and who provides input.

- Adjust the process to include their input into consideration.

- Allow them to participate fully—meaning that they take action items and share accountability.

If Observers persist in interruptions, even while they insist on remaining in an Observer role, insist that the Observer leave.

Create an agenda. The agenda is the plan for accomplishing the goal of the meeting. Like all plans, you may not follow it exactly—adjust based on new information that surfaces in the meeting.

Keep meetings short. We recommend you keep meetings to an hour or less. If you think you need more time, ask yourself if you're trying to accomplish too many goals in one meeting. Remember, people's attention flags during meetings longer than an hour.

Distribute the purpose, agenda, and expected outcomes prior to the meeting. Allow people sufficient time to prepare if preparation is necessary for the meeting. Review and ratify the agenda at the start of the meeting. Allow people to add items or change the priority.

Use a flip-chart page or an agenda on a whiteboard to create the focus for the meeting. Use a template like the one in Figure 8.9, on page 144, to hold the main information about the meeting. Post it in the meeting space so everyone can see the pertinent information at all times. If all the agenda items you need to cover in an hour won't fit on a page using the template above, pare down the agenda or allocate more time.

Capture key information during the meeting. Take notes during the meeting. Notes that everyone can see are most effective. Use a flip chart or whiteboard to capture key points, action times, open issues, and decisions. Some people think it's overkill to write notes on a flip chart or whiteboard. But we've seen too many meetings were each person diligently took private notes—and everyone left the room with a different sense of what happened.

Review outcomes. At the end of the meeting, review action items, decisions, or other outcomes. Determine how the group will follow up on action items. Without a follow-up step, action items are *in*action items.

Distribute notes after the meeting. Transcribe and distribute notes within a day of the meeting. Everyone—core participants and interested parties—should receive notes.

Plan to improve. At the end of every meeting, gather data about how valuable the meeting was for the participants. Use a subjective measure such as Return on Time Invested (ROTI).[4]

Using a five-point scale, ask people to report how much value they received for the time they invested in the meeting (see Figure 8.10, on the facing page).

Post the ratings on a flip chart, and poll the group. Create a histogram that shows the results. An example histogram is shown in Figure 8.11, on the next page.

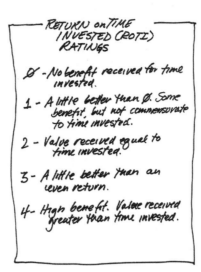

Figure 8.10: RETURN ON INVESTMENT VOTES

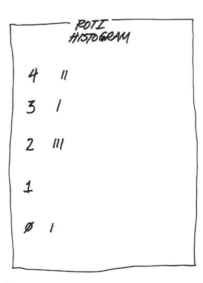

Figure 8.11: RETURN ON INVESTMENT HISTOGRAM

Then ask for information about what made the meeting worthwhile or not worthwhile.

Ask the people who rated the meeting 2 or above what specifically they received for investing their time in the meeting.

Ask people who voted 1 or 0 what they wanted but didn't receive for their investment.

Ask what to keep, what to drop, and what to add for the next similar meeting.

A meeting where a majority of the participants rate the meeting an even return for their time invested is a pretty good meeting.

Ratings below 2 may indicate that there wasn't a match between the people and the purpose, or it may mean the meeting wasn't run well. The additional data gathering should tell you an idea where to improve.

Run Effective Team Meetings

Team meetings help you solve problems and work together as a team, not as a bunch of individuals. Plan on conducting a general team meeting once a week—as long as you have a problem to solve or need to share information among everyone in the group. Make sure your team meetings do not devolve into serial status meetings.

Template:

1. Gossip, Rumors, News

2. Problem-of-the-week (the problem you will work as a team this week)

3. Review action items

Guidelines

We use the same topic headings, but the content will change week-to-week.

- An hour is usually sufficient for this sort of meeting, but you may need more time if you're working on a significant problem.
- Avoid times when people are likely to be sleepy, tired, or ready to leave for the weekend.

- Here are the reasons we ask for rumors, gossip, and good news:
  - Asking for rumors and gossip reduces the power to distract people by making them explicit. Once you are aware of the rumors and gossip, you can fill in the blanks with the real information.
  - Rumors and gossip are an excellent indicator of the mood of the organization, particularly when the organization is under stress.
  - Sharing good news helps improve morale.
- Never ask for individual status in this setting. Individual status is for one-on-ones. Asking for individual status in a group meeting wastes everyone's time. This is different from asking about status on action items that affect the group.
- Focus on solving problems the group needs to solve together. If you're not sure what your group problems are, you can do the following:
  - Ask the group to brainstorm their current list of problems.
  - Review your mission and goals (or, define them).
  - Brainstorm ways your team can be more effective in their work.
- We recommend team meetings be at the same time and location every week. This will help your team form a rhythm of working together.
- Track group-required action items, and work with people individually to monitor their progress and help them, if required.

For an interdependent team, using a fifteen-minute daily stand-up meeting[8] can be very effective. In a daily stand-up, each team member answers three questions:

- What did you do since our last meeting?
- What will you work on today?
- What is getting in your way?

The purpose of a daily stand-up is for the *team* to communicate and commit to each other; ideally, they will direct their answers to each other, not to you, the manager. Keep the meeting short by answering only these three questions. Problem solving happens after the stand-up.

Technique:
Making One-on-Ones Work

One-on-one meetings provide managers an opportunity to ascertain status, solve problems, and provide positive and corrective feedback.

For highly interdependent teams, consider using daily stand-up meetings to create public commitment, improve intrateam communication, and allow for team problem solving (after the stand-up). Use one-on-ones for feedback and coaching, and any other private communication.

Here's the structure we use for a one-on-one meeting:

Greeting. Say "hello." Ask how things are going. This may seem like small talk. It is, and it helps you build rapport.

Discuss status and progress. This is where you find out what people accomplished over the last week, what they didn't accomplish (that they'd planned to), and what their plans are for the next week. Looking at one week in isolation doesn't give you the information you need to know whether the person is getting work done or struggling. When you track status and progress for several weeks in one-on-ones, you can begin to see whether people are having trouble planning, estimating, or accomplishing work.

Obstacles. We ask for obstacles in one-on-ones. We find that if we don't, people suck it up, assume they must soldier on alone, and don't tell us. Removing obstacles is part of a manager's job. So, you need to know what the obstacles are.

Help. Always make a conscious decision about helping. Inflicting help where it isn't needed feels like micromanagement to the victim.

Start by asking whether the person needs help. Help can come in the form of solving problem jointly, generating options, talking through alternatives, pointing to specific information, or simply listening.

Help directly when asked or when department deliverable and goals are in jeopardy.

Career development. Paying attention to your team member's career is another way to build relationships and trust. It shows you are not just there to wring as much work out him or her as possible—you care about his or her career and interests, too. Paying attention to career development will help you keep the best employees.

Anything else to discuss. Leave room for topics your team member wants to address.

Even though you are meeting with people one-on-one, these regular meetings provide an opportunity to observe the dynamics between individuals. Watch for subtle cues of conflict brewing beneath the surface. For example, look for a team member withholding information from others or allowing duplicate work. If you suspect some sabotage or conflict, probe for more information.

If an issue needs resolution, encourage and coach the people who are involved to do so. If they are not able to resolve the issue—even with coaching—then intervene. Resist the temptation to insert yourself in the middle of other people's conflicts.

Review actions (yours and theirs). Summarize and identify any new action items that either of you developed during the one-on-one meeting.

Report on your action items for previous one-on-ones, particularly those that relate to removing obstacles.

Take notes. Take notes during one-on-one meetings. Notes provide a record of the discussions from the previous week and a way to document action items (yours and theirs). Review the previous weeks' notes before each one-on-one meeting—to know what to follow up on, where to probe, and to report on your own action items. Another benefit of keeping notes is that the end of the year, you'll have a record of the entire year. Review the notes prior to year-end discussions to gain a perspective on the entire year.

Troubleshooting one-on-ones. Verbal status reports are likely to be general and vague—"I'm working on the budget" or "It's fine."

After you've been using one-on-ones for a while, people will know how to talk about status and progress. When you start, you may have to coach people on how to organize their work to make status reporting possible and how to keep status visible to you.

Whenever possible, ask your staff to plan in *inch-pebbles*[6]—tasks that deliver something in a day or two. Inch-pebbles keep people focused on producing something tangible and allow you to learn early whether something will take longer than anticipated. Mutually clarify what "done" means for each inch-pebble, and be sure both of you understand your team member's top priorities.

Questions like these help people make their progress visible:

- How will you know when you're done with that?
- What steps will you take?
- Which part will you work on first?
- Can you provide a picture or a measurement of work to date?
- Do you need to collaborate with anyone else on this?
- How will you know you're making progress?
- Who needs to be in the loop if you are unable to finish this on time or run into problems?

If your employees don't show up for their one-on-ones, make sure you've established a standard one-on-one schedule. Meeting every week establishes a rhythm. Maintaining a rhythm when you meet less frequently is difficult. Don't cancel one-on-ones except under the gravest circumstances. Canceling a one-on-one sends the message you don't care—destroying the trust you've built.

Look at how you are conducting the one-on-one. One of the biggest benefits of one-on-ones is building rapport with the people you work with. If your one-on-ones aren't going well, check your own behavior. Are you mostly talking or mostly listening and asking questions?

Make sure you are not taking any other interruptions—phone calls, cell phone calls, pages, email, drop-ins. For example, if *your* boss drops in, politely and firmly say, "I'm in an important meeting now. I'll be with you as soon as it's over." Don't train your boss that it's acceptable to disrespect you and your team member.

Technique:
Preparing for Influence

Most managers cannot succeed in their organization without the cooperation of others. Influence is the art of obtaining cooperation ethically and to mutual benefit. The higher you are in the organization, the more important influencing skills are to your success (and that of your group).

Start with our influence prep sheet shown in Figure 8.12. Answer these questions before you have a conversation where your influence is important.

Guidelines

- Remember that influence is a two-way street.

- Influence is not twisting someone's arm or trying to make them do something against their own best interests.

- Be willing to reciprocate.

What are the other person's interests (their "What's in it for me" WIIFMs)?	
What are the other person's possible losses?	
What are my interests?	
If I had that, what would it do for me?	
Do I have a position? Are there other positions that would meet my interests?	
Where is our common ground?	

Figure 8.12: INFLUENCE PREP SHEET

Technique:
Solving Problems: Create New Situations

Managers solve problems all the time. But solving a problem may simply eliminate an irritant without creating the actual outcome you want. Rather than focus on eliminating the problem, focus on creating the situation you desire. Most of the time, you'll be able to see possible courses of action and select from among them. But sometimes, you need to jump-start your thinking. Start with the steps outlined in Figure 8.13, on the next page.

Guidelines

Follow the template in this order. Seeing the benefits of a solution from others' perspectives can help generate novel solutions.

Understanding barriers can help you build a stronger solution and show where you will need influence and support to succeed. Identify your perceived barriers, and check them with a trusted advisor. You may find your perceived barriers are not as large as you believed.

When you look at the barriers, you may decide you can't change anything, given your position in the organization. Keep working until you find a barrier you can change. For example, if one of your barriers is "unclear corporate priorities," define your own priorities.

Always generate a minimum of three possible ways to achieve the desired situation.

Your first step doesn't need to be a big step for implementing the solution. It should, however, start with an action verb. We say this because we've seen supposed action plans that didn't have verbs! How do you take the first step on an action item like "courage"?

Describe the challenge:

Describe the situation you want to create
(What *do* you want to have instead of the current situation).

Describe how the new situation would benefit:
- You
- The team
- The company

What are the barriers you see:

Generate three possible ways to achieve the new situation (minimum)
Describe which way you recommend, and state the rationale
What's the first step you need to take to? (Start with
an action verb: identify, develop, assess, write, call, etc.)

Figure 8.13: CREATING DESIRED OUTCOME

Technique:
Project Portfolio Planning Tips

You can't commit to any new work without knowing about all the work in your department. We find that without formal project portfolio planning at the department level, people prioritize their own work. Sometimes we find people are working on projects their managers don't know about. If you know what people are working on, and even more important, what's not staffed, you'll know whether you need more people. And, if priorities change, you'll be able to see the effect of those changes on your group quickly.

We use a project portfolio plan that covers the next three to four weeks in detail so that we can see at a glance what people are doing, what's unstaffed, and if priorities need to change, the effect of those priorities. We plan further out than one month but not in much detail. An example of a four-week plan that shows the work going on in one group is shown in Figure 8.14, on the facing page.

Guidelines

- When you gather the universe of work, remember to gather *all* the work:
  - Management work
  - Project work (work toward a specific project with an end date)
  - Periodic work (such as monthly reports or yearly budgets)
  - In-process ad hoc work (work you are doing as the result of crises or other surprises)
  - Ongoing work (support for the operation of an organization or department)
- Break down the pieces of work into small chunks (a week of work or less)
- Name the work specifically. "Coding", by itself, is too high-level a description. "Coding for the XYZ feature for the ABC project" is an appropriate description.
- Make sure people are working on only one project at time and two at the most. The more people switch between projects, the

Week of Person	March 1	March 8	March 15	March 22
Deidre	Feature 1,6 design & development	Feature 7 design & development	bug fixes	bug fixes
Donald	Feature 2,4 design & development	Feature 5 design & devl.	bug fixes	bug fixes
Danny	Feature 3 design & development	bug fixes	operations support	operations support →
Mary manager	Proj. mgmt Group mgmt	→ →	→ budget report	→ →

Note: All work is for Project A
UNSTAFFED WORK - Project B (all of it)

Figure 8.14: EXAMPLE FOUR-WEEK PLAN

less time they have available to work.[2][11] People can work on multiple tasks in the same project, but the more tasks they're supposed to do "simultaneously," the less they will complete.[9]

- Compare the project portfolio against your priorities to see that you're staffing the most important work. Use your mission, your job description, the department's mission, and anything that defines what you're responsible for delivering in your group to define priorities. For example, if your boss says you're responsible for reducing costs, use that responsibility to define how you prioritize the work.
- Every week, add another week to the end of the schedule (and drop the one you've finished). This is the rolling-wave part.
- It's impossible to plan the work in detail months in advance. Plan to replan the work every month or two, and add detail only to the near-term work.
- Use a big visible chart to do the planning and show the results of planning and replanning. Use flip charts, whiteboards,

sticky notes, dots, index cards, and markers. Low-tech tools help people become engaged in planning and communicate that the plan is not immutable and unchanging. Software planning tools don't support rolling-wave plans and don't create the opportunity for people to think about the work as a team.

Bibliography for Chapter

[1] Edward de Bono. *De Bono's Thinking Course, Revised Edition.* Facts on File, Inc., New York, 1994.

[2] Tom DeMarco. *Slack: Getting Past Burnout, Busywork, and the Myth of Total Efficiency.* Broadway Books, New York, 2001.

[3] Esther Derby. "How to Talk About Work Performance: A Feedback Primer." *Crosstalk*, pages 13–16, December 2003.

[4] Esther Derby. "The Roti Method for Gauging Meeting Effectiveness." *Stickyminds.com*, 2003.

[5] Jean McLendon. "The Internal Dialogue in the Consulting Process.", 1985. Unpublished.

[6] Johanna Rothman. "How to Use Inch-Pebbles When You Think You Can't." *Cutter IT Journal*, volume 12(5), May 1999.

[7] Johanna Rothman. *Hiring the Best Knowledge Workers, Techies, and Nerds: The Secrets and Science of Hiring Technical People.* Dorset House, New York, 2004.

[8] Ken Schwaber. *Agile Project Management with Scrum.* Microsoft Press, Redmond, WA, 2004.

[9] Joel Spolsky. *Joel on Software: And on Diverse and Occasionally Related Matters That Will Prove of Interest to Software Developers, Designers, and Managers, and to Those Who, Whether by Good Fortune or Ill Luck, Work with Them in Some Capacity.* Apress, Berkeley, CA, 2004.

[10] Brian R. Stanfield. *The Workshop Book: From Individual Creativity to Group Action (Ica Series).* New Society Publishing, Gabriola Island, BC, 2002.

[11] Gerald M. Weinberg. *The Secrets of Consulting.* Dorset House, New York, 1985.

Bibliography

Lou Adler. *Hire with Your Head: Using Power Hiring to Build Great Companies*. John Wiley & Sons, Hoboken, NJ, 2002.

Mary Albright and Clay Carr. *101 Biggest Mistakes Managers Make*. Prentice Hall, New York, 1997.

Robert R. Blake and Jane Srygley Mouton. *The Versatile Manager: A Grid Profile*. Dow Jones-Irwin, Homewood, IL, 1980.

Kenneth Blanchard and Spencer Johnson. *The One Minute Manager*. Berkeley Publishing Group, New York, 1982.

Michael Bolton. "Are You Ready?" *STQE*, pages 50–54, May 2003.

David L. Bradford and Allen R. Cohen. *Managing for Excellence: The Guide to Developing High Performance in Contemporary Organizations.*. John Wiley & Sons, New York, 1984.

Frederick P. Brooks, Jr. *The Mythical Man Month: Essays on Software Engineering*. Addison-Wesley, Reading, MA, anniversary edition, 1995.

W. Steven Brown. *Thirteen Fatal Errors Managers Make and How You Can Avoid Them*. Berkley Books, New York, 1985.

Marcus Buckingham and Curt Coffman. *First, Break All the Rules: What the World's Greatest Managers Do Differently*. Simon and Schuster, New York, NY, 1999.

Clay Carr. *The New Manager's Survival Guide: All the Skills You Need for Success, 2nd Edition*. John Wiley & Sons, New York, 1995.

Sidney J. Chapman. "Hours of Labour." *Economic Journal*, pages 363–65, September 1909. Footnote 1.

Robert Cialdini. "Perplexing Problem? Borrow Some Brains." *Harvard Management Communication Letter*, August 2004.

Tom Coens and Mary Jenkins. *Abolishing Performance Appraisals: Why They Backfire and What to Do Instead.* Barrertt-Koehler, San Francisco, 2002.

Allen R. Cohen and David L. Bradford. *Influence without Authority.* John Wiley & Sons, New York, 1991.

Stephen R. Covey. *Principle-Centered Leadership.* Summit Books, New York, 1991.

Edward de Bono. *De Bono's Thinking Course, Revised Edition.* Facts on File, Inc., New York, 1994.

Tom DeMarco. *Slack: Getting Past Burnout, Busywork, and the Myth of Total Efficiency.* Broadway Books, New York, 2001.

Tom Demarco and Timothy Lister. *Peopleware: Productive Projects and Teams.* Dorset House, New York, NY, second edition, 1999.

Esther Derby. "Climbing the Learning Curve: Practice with Feedback." *Insights*, 2002. Fall.

Esther Derby. "If at First, and Last, You Don't Succeed." *STQE*, volume 4(5), September 2002.

Esther Derby. "How to Talk About Work Performance: A Feedback Primer." *Crosstalk*, pages 13–16, December 2003.

Esther Derby. "Managing a Struggling Employee." *Insights*, 2003.

Esther Derby. "The Roti Method for Gauging Meeting Effectiveness." *Stickyminds.com*, 2003.

Esther Derby. "Hiring for a Collaborative Team." *Computerworld.com*, April 2004. http://www.computerworld.com.

Esther Derby. "A Real Go-Getter." *STQE*, volume 5(4), September 2004.

Esther Derby. "Setting Clear Priorities." *Computerworld.com*, January 2004.

Esther Derby. "What Your Weekly Meetings Aren't Telling You." *Better Software*, volume 3(6):pages 40–41, March 2004.

Peter Drucker. *Managing for Results.* Pan Books, London, 1964.

Gerald W. Faust, Richard I. Lyles, and Will Phillips. *Responsible Managers Get Results: How the Best Find Solutions—Not Excuses.* American Management Association, New York, 1998.

Daniel Feldman. *The Manager's Pocket Guide to Workplace Coaching*. HRD Press, Amherst, MA, 2001.

Gene Fellner, editor. *Unreported and Upaid Overtime: Distorted Measurements and Formulas for Failure*. Pearson Education, Boston, 2002.

Roger Fisher, William Ury, and Bruce Patton. *Getting to Yes, Second ed*. Penguin Books, New York, 1991.

Ferdinand F. Fournies. *Coaching for Improved Work Performance*. McGraw Hill, New York, 2000.

John J. Gabarro and John P. Kotter. "Managing Your Boss." *Harvard Business Review*, pages 92–100, January 1980.

Sumantra Ghoshal Heike Bruch. "What Your Weekly Meetings Aren't Telling You." *Harvard Business Review*, volume 80(2), February 2002.

Linda A. Hill. *Becoming a Manager: How New Managers Master the Challenge of Leadership*. Penguin Group, New York, 1992.

Tom Janz, Lowell Hellerik, and David C. Gilmore. *Behavior Description Interviewing*. Prentice-Hall, Englewood Cliffs, NJ, 1986.

Sam Kaner. *The Facilitator's Guide to Participatory Decision-Making*. New Society Publishers, Gabriola Island, BC, 1996.

Naomi Karten. *Communication Gaps and How to Close Them*. Dorset House, New York, 2002.

Jon R. Katzenbach and Douglas K. Smith. *The Wisdom of Team: Creating the High-Performance Organization*. HarperCollins Publishers, New York, 1999.

Patrick Lencioni. *The Five Dysfunctions of a Team: A Leadership Fable*. Jossey-Bass, A Wiley Company, San Francisco, 2002.

Joan Magretta and Nan Stone. *What Management Is: How It Works and Why It's Everyone's Business*. Free Press, New York, NY, 2002.

Steve McConnell. *Rapid Development: Taming Wild Software Schedules*. Microsoft Press, Redmond, WA, 1996.

Patrick J. McKenna and David H. Maister. *First among Equals: How to Manage a Group of Professionals*. The Free Press, New York, 2002.

Jean McLendon. "The Internal Dialogue in the Consulting Process.", 1985. Unpublished.

Thomas J. Peters and Robert H. Jr. Waterman. *In Search of Excellence: Lessons from America's Best-Run Companies*. Warner Books, New York, 1982.

Johanna Rothman. "How to Use Inch-Pebbles When You Think You Can't." *Cutter IT Journal*, volume 12(5), May 1999.

Johanna Rothman. "Project Portfolio Management 101." *Business-IT Alignment E-Mail Advisor*, October 2001.

Johanna Rothman. "No More Meeting Mutinies." *Software Development*, March 2002.

Johanna Rothman. "Practice, a Necessary Part of Change." *Cutter IT Email Advisorory*, February 2002.

Johanna Rothman. "Tips for Passing the Baton." *Software Development*, February 2002.

Johanna Rothman. "Successful Software Management: Fourteen Lessons Learned." *Crosstalk*, pages 17–20, December 2003.

Johanna Rothman. *Corrective Action for the Software Industry*. Paton Press, Chico, CA, 2004.

Johanna Rothman. *Hiring the Best Knowledge Workers, Techies, and Nerds: The Secrets and Science of Hiring Technical People*. Dorset House, New York, 2004.

Ken Schwaber. *Agile Project Management with Scrum*. Microsoft Press, Redmond, WA, 2004.

Charles Seashore, Edith Seashore, and Gerald M. Weinberg. *What Did You Say? The Art of Giving and Receiving Feedback*. Bingham House Books, Columbia, MD, 1997.

Peter Senge. *The Fifth Discipline: The Art and Practice of the Learning Organization*. Currency/Doubleday, New York, NY, 1990.

Joel Spolsky. *Joel on Software: And on Diverse and Occasionally Related Matters That Will Prove of Interest to Software Developers, Designers, and Managers, and to Those Who, Whether by Good Fortune or Ill Luck, Work with Them in Some Capacity*. Apress, Berkeley, CA, 2004.

Brian R. Stanfield. *The Workshop Book: From Individual Creativity to Group Action (Ica Series)*. New Society Publishing, Gabriola Island, BC, 2002.

Gerald M. Weinberg. *The Secrets of Consulting*. Dorset House, New York, 1985.

Gerald M. Weinberg. *Becoming a Technical Leader: An Organic Problem-Solving Approach*. Dorset House, New York, 1986.

Gerald M. Weinberg. *Quality Software Management: Volume 1, Systems Thinking*. Dorset House Publishing, Inc., New York, 1992.

Gerald M. Weinberg. *Quality Software Management, Volume 3: Congruent Action*. Dorset House, New York, 1994.

XP Universe. *Brokering With eXtreme Programming*, 2001. http://www.agileuniverse.com/2001/pdfs/EP201.pdf.

Index

Help for the Whole Team

Congratulations on joining the world-wide Pragmatic community. Together, we can make a difference to **developers** and their **managers** interested in a better way.

Here are some of our other Pragmatic Bookshelf titles that you and your team may enjoy.

Ship It!

This book shows you how to run a software project and *Ship It!*, on time and on budget, without excuses. You'll learn the common technical infrastructure that every project needs along with well-accepted, easy-to-adopt, best-of-breed practices that really work, as well as common problems and how to solve them.

Ship It!: A Practical Guide to Successful Software Projects
Jared Richardson and Will Gwaltney
(200 pages) ISBN: 0-9745140-4-7. $29.95

My Job Went to India

The job market is shifting. Your current job may be outsourced, perhaps to India or eastern Europe. But you can save your job and improve your career by following these practical and timely tips. See how to: • treat your career as a business • build your own personal brand • develop a structured plan for keeping your skills up to date • market yourself to your company and rest of the industry • keep your job!

My Job Went to India: 52 Ways to Save Your Job
Chad Fowler
(230 pages) ISBN: 0-9766940-1-8. $19.95

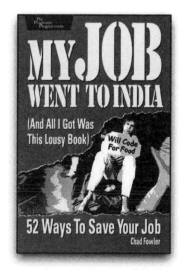

The Pragmatic Bookshelf

The Pragmatic Bookshelf features books written by working practitioners. The titles continue the well-known Pragmatic Programmer style, and continue to garner awards and rave reviews. As software development gets more and more difficult, the Pragmatic Programmers will be there with more titles and products to help programmers and their managers stay on top of their game.

Visit Us Online

Behind Closed Doors Home Page
pragmaticprogrammer.com/titles/rdbcd
Web home for this book, where you can find and submit errata, send us feedback, and find other related resources.

Register for Updates
pragmaticprogrammer.com/updates
Be notified when updates and new books become available.

Join the Community
pragmaticprogrammer.com/community
Read our weblogs, join our online discussions, participate in our mailing list, interact with our wiki, and benefit from the experience of other Pragmatic Programmers.

New and Noteworthy
pragmaticprogrammer.com/news
Check out the latest pragmatic developments in the news.

Save on the PDF

Save 50% on the PDF version of this book. Owning the paper version of this book entitles you to purchase the PDF version for only $8.25 (regularly $16.50). That's a saving of 50%. The PDF is great for carrying around on your laptop. It's hyperlinked and is fully searchable. Buy it now at pragmaticprogrammer.com/coupon

Contact Us

Phone Orders:	1-800-699-PROG (+1 919 847 3884)
Online Orders:	www.pragmaticprogrammer.com/catalog
Customer Service:	orders@pragmaticprogrammer.com
Non-English Versions:	translations@pragmaticprogrammer.com
Pragmatic Teaching:	academic@pragmaticprogrammer.com
Author Proposals:	proposals@pragmaticprogrammer.com